CHURCH GROWTH
FROM THE GROUND UP

CHURCH GROWTH
FROM THE GROUND UP

First Edition

To: LaToya
God Bless Thanks

Bishop Dortch

Bishop Derrick Dortch

Library of Congress Control Number:		2010901466
ISBN:	Hardcover	978-1-4500-3797-6
	Softcover	978-1-4500-3796-9
	EBook	978-1-4500-3798-3

To order additional copies of this book, contact:
Xlibris Corporation
1-888-795-4274
www.Xlibris.com
Orders@Xlibris.com
65672

SPECIAL THANKS

Writing my first book was a huge undertaking for me. It required intense focus and a lot of time. Certainly, it required keen understanding from my precious wife and children, notably called my partners in ministry. Truly my wife has been the backbone of support for this project, and I am ever grateful for her contribution in my life. I would like to take this time to thank them for their contribution of understanding, allowing me the time away to complete this project.

I would also like to thank my church family who kept the flames of excitement surrounding this project burning. Because of their support of time, talent, and treasure, they truly make it easy to be me. Most of all, I would like to thank God for giving me the grace and strength to complete such a great assignment.

About the Author

Bishop Dortch is the senior pastor of the Faith Cathedral Church. Bishop Dortch was baptized and filled with the Holy Ghost in September of 1989. Previously, he was a victim of gang violence and was running the inner-city streets of Chicago. Now he serves as a testimony of life, telling the good news of the glorious Gospel everywhere he goes. He has a BA in business administration and is trained in organizational management. Bishop Dortch is married to his beautiful wife Kimmular Dortch, for nearly 16 years. They are the proud parents of five beautiful children; Amber, Ericka, Derrick Jr, Brittany, and Daniel.

After receiving the call of God, he founded this great church, Faith Cathedral Church, in May of 2002 with just eight adults and a few children. Since then, God has stamped his approval on the ministry and continues to add to this church on a weekly basis. Bishop Dortch is an anointed visionary with a heart for the people of God. In this book, he shares his heart about what it means to found a church from the ground up. Join in and be blessed.

CONTENTS

Introduction 11

Properly Examining Your Call 15
Overcoming Misconceptions...23
Establishing the Church's Agenda...................................32
    Teaching Social Responsibility to Members 35
    Developing a Team Mentality....................................44
    Providing Direction to the Faithful............................47

The Visitor: Most Important Member of the Church 49
Keys to Effective Evangelism 51
    The Invite 51

The Kingdom Invitation 56
    The Law of Numbers...57
    Growth Plan 59
    Conversion Growth Rate..61
    Establishing Faith Goals..62

Services...65
    Timeliness...66
    Opening of the Service 68
    Pulpit Educate 70
    Offerings...71
    Preaching 74
    Altar Call 78
    Dismissal...79

Follow Up a Key Element 81

Follow-up Process 82
The Visitor Form 83

Presence of the Spirit 90
Avoiding the Trap of Pride 91
Avoid the Sabotage of Sexual Impurity 92
Lust Plan 95

God Is in the Soul-saving Business 98
Church Growth Elements 99
Family and Friends Day 99

Outreach Campaigns 101
Launching the Outreach Campaign 102
Teaching 103
Marketing 104
Passion 105
Making a Confident Altar Call 106

Faith 107
Process of Faith 110
Faith Props 113
Applying Faith to My Church Growth 115

Humble Beginning 116
Getting the "I" Out 117
Learning How to Do Church 117

Closing Tips 118

Reference Tools 120
Phone Scripts

INTRODUCTION

This manuscript is being designed for the benefit and direction of pastors and their parishioners who have been in existence for less than ten years. Of course, we welcome all churches to glean from the content of this book; however, it is specifically designed to provide direction for churches and pastors who are fresh off the block.

I started Faith Cathedral Church seven years ago at the Fox Center located in Oak Park, Illinois. I never will forget the Sundays that I woke up wondering who would show up at service that Sunday. As a matter of fact, this proved to be my biggest fear. Being in a fairly large church (three hundred plus members) for so many years, I had become accustomed to having a good number of people in church. Now I was traumatized looking at an audience of about eight adults and ten children every Sunday morning. During midweek Bible class, things got worse. I remember times when only one person would show up for Bible class. These were times of great discouragement for me as a new pastor.

For years now, the Spirit of God has dealt with my heart concerning this element of ministry. I am intrigued with how churches are built and the special training that each pastor so desperately needs. It is certainly my hope and prayer that this book will serve as a ministry tool for young churches all over the world.

Before I started pastoring, I knew the call of God was on my life. Like most young pastors, I felt it was my time or my season, as some say. Like most young pastors, God had given me great confirmation and assurance that this was his leading in my life. However, once I got in the waters of pastoring, I quickly learned I did not know how to swim.

So there I was every week with my wife and children looking at me in the face. My family faithfully sat there, wishing me well and supporting me with all their hearts. I truly thought I knew what to do. In my mind, I believed in a few short weeks the church would be filled. After all, once people heard me preach, how could they not want to come back and join? Well, as that old expression goes, "Legend in my own mind." That's what I was, a legend in my own mind. I think that most pastors suffer from this when they first get started.

There were some other good people who decided to stand with me during that season. I will always be grateful for the contribution of time, dedication, and support that they gave. God allowed them to stand with me in one of the most difficult times in my pastoral era. Again, I am forever grateful to them as they helped me get started.

I'm writing this book to every young pastor who finds himself in this situation. Growing a church from the ground up or starting with very few members is a very difficult task. This book will by no means take the difficultness out of the process, but it will provide healthy direction for growing your church.

> A wise man will hear, and will increase learning; and a man of understanding shall attain unto wise counsels. (Prov. 1:5)

The body of Christ is filled with wonderful men and women of God, especially those that dare to embrace the call of being a pastor. However, because of the lack of training, tutoring, and teaching, many pastors waste precious years learning what to do. The fact that you have purchased this book is a great indication that you desire to learn. Whether you are a pastor or have been called to stand alongside your pastor, this is a great read. I believe it will be encouraging and exciting to all.

Most of all, this book will answer some questions. Questions like the following:

How can my church be effective even while we are so small?

What should outreach and evangelism look like in my church when we are small?

Is there any training and direction that will be helpful to me?

Is it possible for my church to really grow?

These questions and more will be answered in the pages ahead. I truly believe your reading this book is not an accident. God has ordered it in your life at the right time. Get ready to be blessed!

Properly Examining Your Call

Most pastors spend so much time hiding behind the real issues. However, the real issues need addressing if our pastoring tenor is going to be rewarding. There are two major questions that I would like you to consider.

The first question is, why did you start your church? This is of grave importance. Please note I'm not the judge or jury on this issue; however, it is a real issue that must be resolved in your heart. Did God really call you to pastor? Again, I'm not the judge or jury, but if pastoring will be rewarding, this is something that must be solid in your faith.

Some pastors truly started pastoring with the wrong motive, and motive to the call is crucial. For example, did you leave and start your church because you were mad at the church you left? Now be true to yourself, because God already knows why you did it, especially if he was not in it. If you did, go back and apologize to your home church regardless of the situation. The reason this is so important is you can't pastor people out of hurt. Neither can you pastor people when you are mad.

> In Mark 11:25, Jesus said, "And when ye stand praying, forgive, if ye have ought against any: that your Father also which is in heaven may forgive you your trespasses.

"You must be willing to forgive. You heart needs to be clear and free from all issues that can be a potential distraction. You being able to minister the Word freely without reservation is of grave importance.

Did you start the church because of competition? Just because someone you knew started a church and is doing fairly well does not mean you can. You can't make the mistake of saying, "If they did, I can too." That's not true. Remember, you must be called to the office of a pastor. This is not ambition or some type of business venture. This is the precious anointed responsibility of dealing and handling God's most precious commodity: his people. In Jeremiah 3:15, the Lord speaks these words:

> "And I will give you pastors according to My heart, which shall feed you with knowledge and understanding."

This is not something we can guess about or take a chance on. The call to the office of pastor is very serious. Look at Jeremiah 12:10. God says, "Many Pastors have destroyed My vineyard, they have trodden My portion underfoot, they have made My pleasant portion a desolate wilderness." This scripture speaks of leaders who have failed to take the call of God serious.

In Jeremiah 23:1, the Lord says, "Woe unto the Pastors who destroy and scatter the sheep of My pasture! Saith the Lord."

I've placed these scriptures in here to further solidify the seriousness of the call. Please understand I'm not the judge or the jury on this issue. I'm merely trying to help you see how your heart has to be positioned if God is going to trust you with his jewels. Yes, God's people are jewels. Jesus calls the body of Christ his bride.

Remember, you need to be free from all issues of the heart and able to minister God's Word freely without distraction. You need to preserve the name and the smell of your ministry within your local city. Face it, when someone mentions the name of your church, you would like that conversation to be a good one.

A good name is precious and must be guarded and protected. It could prove very important for your outreach efforts in ministry. As pastors, we must be totally clear of anything and anybody that will distract us from our call. You should know God called you. You should know what your individual assignment to the body of Christ is. Lastly, you should know where the anointing within your ministry works best. Some churches are anointed in the area of teaching or preaching, and some in the area of singing and administration. Find what works for your church and start building upon what God has given you.

There is one last thing I would like to add concerning the start of any church. Just because you are having a difficult time does not mean God did not call you. There might just be one or two things you need to change. Additionally, just because you may not have many people at the current moment is no indication that God did not call you. Maybe your current members are not inviting enough people to come. Don't use that as a spiritual thermometer to gauge whether or not your church is hot or cold, good or bad. That's a mistake waiting to happen to you. Mobilize your people to start inviting people. We will discuss this in greater detail in a later chapter.

Yes, we know that there will be people who have never pastored a church criticize you and have immature remarks concerning your growth. However, don't allow their words to discourage you. Remember, you must start somewhere. If you give up just because of a little trouble, then you should have never started. Building a church from the ground up is not an easy assignment. However, when God calls, he is obligated to make provision for the vision.

Never compare your church growth or nongrowth with someone else's. Time can easily bring about a change. We have seen churches with large memberships drop and churches with small memberships explode. Unjust comparisons are a tool that the devil will use to hold over your head and discourage you. If you are not careful, he will have you comparing everything others are doing while you should be trying to perfect that which God has given you to do.

This is a mistake that most members of a church will make. They will constantly prompt you to do what another church is doing. Although there is nothing wrong with embracing best practices from other churches, please don't allow this to stop you from perfecting what your church currently has. To all members, if God has called you to stand alongside your men or women of God, please understand your perfecting responsibilities. You must perfect what you currently have before you can properly embrace new methods. If your pastor is a good teacher, promote his teaching. If he is an excellent preacher, promote his preaching. If your pastor can sing, let the world know you have a man or woman of God who can sing. Perfect it, perfect it, and perfect it! Make sure the microphones are ready, ushers are in place, and the service runs smoothly. Perfect that which you currently have, and it will set the stage for embracing new direction from God.

The second important question that I would like to examine is, do you want your church to grow?

Church growth is a critical part of any church. If you want your church to grow, then you are going to have to spend time understanding what others did to grow their churches. Churches grow on purpose, not by chance. It takes planned purposeful effort for churches to grow. Down through the years, I've often heard people refer to this scripture.

In Psalm 127:1, the scripture says, "Except the Lord build the house, they labour in vain who build it: except the Lord keep the city, the watchman wakes but in vain."

I think they stretched it too far. In years past, they almost made it seem like we were not supposed to do any labor because God was going to build his house.

However, we must have a full understanding of this psalm. This is a family psalm (believed to be written by Solomon) dedicated to Solomon by his father. David, having a house to build and a city to keep, directs Solomon to look up to God and to depend totally on his providence, warning him if he did not depend upon God, all of his wisdom, care, and industry would not serve him.

In principle, this applies to every area of life. However, in soul winning and church growth, we certainly have a part to play. This scripture, although in principle is true, should not be used as an excuse for non-outreach activity within our churches. We will look at this more closely in another chapter.

Church growth is a question that should be asked of every pastor as well as his or her members. It should be the collective purpose of the church, winning souls for Jesus Christ.

I don't know about you, but I was reared to look at mega churches very negatively. Most of the comments from the pulpits of smaller churches were "People are doing anything just to get members or numbers." You may have heard this statement before. Well, I found out that that's not completely true. As I prepared to write this book, I found it necessary to understand the plight of the mega church, since this is the plateau of church success for many. Here's what I found out.

Mega churches are doing a great work for God. In fact, many of their leaders have learned how to walk by faith. They have used their faith to reap great blessings in ministry. In Hebrews 11:6, the scripture says, "But without Faith it is impossible to please Him: for he who comes to God must believe that He is and that he is a rewarder of them who diligently seek Him."

Most, not all, of the mega church leaders are men and women of faith. They are very disciplined and purposeful in their efforts. They are completely sold-out to the ministry that God has called them to. Additionally, they have many people in their churches who are spirit-filled believers, living righteous lives before God.

As I came to understand the story of the mega church leader, I learned that many of them served God broke, without adequate financial support for many years. This helped me understand that for them, it was not just about the money. In fact, they had no idea God would bless them the way he has. Without proper understanding of their story, it's difficult to handle the glory that God has placed upon them.

With a large or mega church, there are many diverse people who were reared in different fashions regarding sanctification and holiness. However, please remember that these people have the same testimonies as the people in the smaller churches. They have been delivered from drugs, fornication, partying, and the like. God's delivering power is just as present, big or small.

Some pastors are not able to handle more than a hundred people, while others are able to handle five thousand people. God knows what we can handle and either blesses us accordingly or enlarges our hearts to handle more. Pride is a key issue for leaders. I like what the Apostle Paul says in 2 Corinthians 12:7:

> "And lest I should be exalted above measure through the abundance of Revelations there was given to me a thorn in the flesh, the messenger of Satan to buffet me, lest I should be exalted above measure."

In other words, God allowed him to be afflicted so that the great revelations God had given him would not ruin him and cause him to be prideful. Many of us, if God gave us a mega church right away (key emphasis *right away*), we would not be able to handle it. So while God is growing the church, he is also growing us.

This reminds me of another statement that I've heard down through the years. "I would rather have ten people who are truly saved than to have ten thousand that are not saved."

I discovered that these statements and others like it proved to shape my thinking concerning church growth and larger churches. Now that I'm pastoring, I've discovered the total opposite. Most pastors would rather have ten thousand who are not saved versus the ten who are saved. I totally agree, because with ten thousand unsaved, you have a chance to do a greater work for the Lord. Although the statement above sounds really pious and holy, it's not biblical. No pastor in his or her right mind wants to be in church with just ten people. After a prolonged situation, the pastor and the people will be far too discouraged to continue. The church would be totally unhealthy and on the verge of dying.

Let me remind you of a few scriptures in the New Testament.

In Acts 2:41, three thousand souls were added to the church.

In Acts 4:4, five thousand souls were added to the church.

In Acts 13:44, almost the whole city came to hear the Word of God.

These scriptures alone should tell you what God thinks about church growth. God is certainly not a stranger to the mega church; after all, he designed it and made it so. He started the church off with large numbers and expanded it all over the world.

Most times when we talk about church growth, pastors get nervous wondering what kind of compromising they will have to do in order to grow their church. Some of the things we call compromise should have never been on the table in the first place. We must be honest as pastors and set healthy boundaries in our churches according to godly principles. Certainly you can take anything too far. However, I am truly convinced that traditions are not the major things that will cause your church not to grow.

Listen, I've done my homework in this area. There are churches of other persuasion (non-Christians) who embrace all kinds of traditions and their faiths grow. For reasons of presentation, I will not name any particular group. However, look outside of your box and think. Then there are churches without traditions that experience great growth. Equally, there are churches who embrace traditions but never grow. Also, there are churches who embrace traditions and experience great growth. Long story short, whether or not you have traditions or not is not the most vital factor to church growth.

The most vital factor is this: if a church is not busy witnessing, inviting, and providing healthy ministry within the church, it will not grow. It makes no difference whether you have traditions or not; if there is no outreach activities taking place, your church will not grow.

This has been an issue of great debate over the years. As it relates to church growth, I would encourage every pastor and member to focus on the assignment God has given to you. Do not allow yourself to become distracted with this issue. God is in the business of winning souls and so should you.

Now please think about what I'm about to say. There are groups all over the world from many different denominations and teachings, many of which make no sense to the Christian believer, yet they grow. Now the most popular answer to this question is this: the devil fights the real church worse than these other groups. I concur this is true. But the real question is, what are they doing to cause people to come through their doors? In order to grow, you must have the ability to bring people in the doors. Can you see my point? How do I get people to come into my doors?

This is the area that we must understand and become developed in doing. When I have people coming through my doors, then I have a chance for church growth. If I get comfortable preaching to the same people, the devil will rock me to sleep and stagnate God's church. When we are in contact with people, we have a chance. If members are not working to bring people through the doors, we will not grow. If we grow, it will be small and isolated spurts that happen occasionally. Pastors and members who desire church growth understand we can't take that chance. We need purposeful effort if we are going to be effective.

Please understand if you are going to pastor people, you need people. I know that statement sounds very simple, but it's so true. You can't be a pastor with no people. With that in mind, you must get in the habit of giving people a cause to come to your church. Then you must have an outreach regiment designed to keep people coming into the doors of your church. This is something that other groups understand and have been exceptionally good at doing. They are so committed to the cause and what they do that it works. In principle, diligence pays off. These groups are diligent, and it pays off. I would like to add that many of the other groups that I considered are not even spirit filled.

It blows my mind when I see other persuasions whose services are packed every week. Upon further examination, I looked at their efforts for outreach and it's awesome. Now think about this: we have a real savior and a divine commission from Jesus to work in our father's vineyard. In consideration of this, I believe our churches should be growing week by week. In order to do this, we must overcome some of the misconceptions that we have inherited.

Overcoming Misconceptions

There are some great misconceptions that we as pastors of growing churches must understand and overcome. I'm not sure where we got them from, but we must rid ourselves of these misconceptions so that we can truly experience the growth that God has planned for us.

I'm going to list them in numbered order and deal with each misconception individually. Here is the first one.

1. All I have to do is pray and God is going to send in my increase.

This might sound a bit commercial, but in many instances, it's true. Some pastors believe that God is going to just send people into their churches without any evangelical efforts at all. All they have to do is live holy and pray. That's not what Jesus told us to do. Praying and living holy is not an outreach duty. Praying and living holy should be a relationship duty to God regardless of what endeavor you are trying to accomplish.

In Luke 14:23, Jesus says, "And the Lord said unto the servant, 'Go out into the highways and hedges, and compel them to come in, that my house may be filled.'"

He gave these instructions to the church. This is what real outreach is all about. Mobilizing your members, whether you have ten or two hundred, to invite/compel people to come in. Notice the later clause of the verse. God wants his house full. He does not want it full just during your church convention or anniversary times. He wants it filled during regular Sunday morning service.

When I look at the instructions that Jesus gave to his disciples, it encourages my heart to understand that outreach is a necessary part of church growth. This misconception has staggered many good pastors who were overspiritual and out of touch with the instructions of the scripture. It is that will of God that your church grows. Can you see that? Even if you are just a member reading this book, please be reminded you must invite/compel people to come in.

Now let's look at misconception number 2.

2. I am so anointed that once the people hear my preaching, they will stay.

All pastors, whether they admit it or not, at one point believed that they had the world's revelation. In other words, what God had given them was not taking place anywhere else.

Additionally, once people hear what they had to say, they are going to be converted and stay in the church. In fact, many of us are stuck on our preaching and teaching. We might have a few others that like our preaching and teaching, and it massages our egos and causes us to get stuck.

The real truth of the matter is you're just another preacher or teacher in the body of Christ. Also, God does not give it all to one person. So don't get stuck on yourself. Grow out of this mind-set as it will cause you to become prideful, and God will not be able to use you. When we get stuck on ourselves, then we are certainly not relying on the Spirit of God. Remember, God is not going to compete with your ego.

As pastors, members, and leaders, we must remember if we are going to be great, God is going to have to do it. It will never come as a result of self-promotion. Look at this scripture.

> So then neither is he that planteth anything, neither he that watereth; but God that giveth the increase. (1 Cor. 3:7)

I remember the Lord taught me a very valuable lesson once. One Sunday, God moved upon me, and the Spirit of God was overwhelming in our church service that morning. We had quite a few visitors that Sunday. When the altar call was made, every one of them that tried to come to the altar was slain in the Spirit, literally falling down even before I could pray or minister to them. God truly allowed the Holy Ghost to have his way in our midst. The saints were excited because we never had so many visitors touched at one time. I can clearly remember leaving the service that day saying to myself, *After a day like today, I know those people are coming back.*

Well, even to this day, I have not seen those people anymore. Case in point, God is the only one that can truly bring increase. Equally, we had a Sunday when it appeared that the Holy Ghost was not as strong in the service. The visitors present did not even come to the altar that Sunday. I was under the impression that they did not enjoy the service. To my surprise, they came back next Sunday and have been with us even to this day. They are baptized, spirit-filled believers now and have grown mightily in the Lord.

Case in point, it's not by might nor by power, but by the Spirit of the Lord. It's not going to be you; it's always God. So now I've learned never to depend upon my preaching or teaching. All I do is plant and water; that's my job. The real increase comes from God. Sounds real simple, but it's a great revelation to be considered. You need to give God a studied mind, a rested body, and a willing spirit, then watch him work.

Now, let's look at misconception number 3.

3. I don't need any help; all I need is Jesus.

Well, this is simply not true. You will need other people to help you. You need people to do praise and worship, testimony service, etc. You will need people to lift offerings, usher, and nurse. You will need other churches for fellowship. You will need other leaders to be an ear in times of discouragement and a voice for encouragement. Long story short, you will need people to help you fulfill the call of God in your life.

This reminds me of a very funny story. There was once a pastor who kept preaching "I don't need nobody, all I need is Jesus." This pastor would really preach this hard. Well, the church was already small and struggling without many people there. Yet this pastor was hard and difficult, quick to let people know "I don't need you." Well, in the process of time, the few people they had left. One Sunday morning, there was no one to preach to, and the cry was made. "Oh God, where are the people?"

Then the Lord replied, "Preach to me, I'm here."

Again, let's be honest. You can't be an effective pastor without God's people. Please don't get nervous because I used the word *need*. I'm not saying that any leader needs any one person. Neither am I saying that pastors should be afraid and allow people to back them up in a corner. By the way, a real saint would not want to be that immature anyway. All I'm trying to illustrate is that you will need help. Let's face it, when we go to church, it's no fun just preaching to Jesus. Look at this scripture.

> And they went forth, and preached every where, the Lord working with them, and confirming the word with signs following. (Mark 16:20)

Notice the word *they* in that scripture. It did not say I or me. It always says them or they, indicating more than one. Now draw your attention to the words of this scripture that says "the Lord working with them." God worked with them as they worked. It did not say God worked with him or her; it says "them."

Notice also that God worked with them. It did not say God did all the work while they sat somewhere, praying and living holy. It did not say, "The Lord built the house as they sat idle, praying." No, it says God worked with them, confirming what they said, with signs following. So the principle is, if you work, God will work with you. Once more, please notice the words *they* or *them*, not *I* or *him*. This means more than one. Case in point, you need help.

Now, let's look at another misconception.

4. I don't need any training. God is going to show me how to do everything.

This is one of the greatest misconceptions that I see many young pastors make. There is a training aspect to ministry; whether formal or informal, you will need some training. Training for most pastors has only been working in the normal departments of the church that they have been raised in. It typically involves addressing a crowd to preach or officiating a service, which, for the most part, is great.

However, there is some other training that I believe is necessary for effective church growth. When we start telling pastors about the need for training, most of us feel belittled. Training makes us feel like we are missing something or we are inadequate for the task. It becomes a great push against our pride and ego, depending upon how we perceive our need for training.

Let me remind you of all the training that went on in the Bible. In my first example, let's look at Moses and Joshua in Numbers 27:18-23:

> And the Lord said unto Moses, Take thee Joshua the son of Nun, a man in whom is the Spirit, and lay your hand upon him. And set him before Eleazar the Priest, and before the entire congregation; and give him a charge in their sight. And you shall put some of your honour upon him, that all the congregation of the Children of Israel may be obedient. And he shall stand before Eleazar the Priest, who shall ask counsel for him after the judgment of Urim before the Lord; at his word shall they go out, and at his word they shall come in, both he, and all the Children of Israel with him, even all the congregation. And Moses did as the Lord commanded him; and he took Joshua, and set him before Eleazar the Priest, and before the entire congregation; And he laid his hands upon him, and gave him a charge, as the Lord commanded by the hand of Moses.

Please take note of the instructions God gave Moses. God told Moses to stand Joshua before the congregation and give him charge in their sight. Then God tells Moses, "Put some of your honor upon him." This sounds like training to me. It sounds as if Joshua had never had the opportunity to stand before the priest, and at his word, the people would go out or come in.

Notice God tells Moses to put some of his honor upon Joshua. I really like that because it lets me know, as pastor, we have honor, and we can put honor on others as instructed by God. Again, my point is the training. God knew Joshua would need some things. In verse 20, it says so that the children of Israel may be obedient. God is a god of order. He knew Joshua needed some training, and God made sure it happened.

Let's look at another example: Elijah and Elisha. Elijah found Elisha plowing with a team of oxen between the Sea of Galilee and the Dead Sea on the western side of the Jordan River. As Elijah walked past Elisha, he threw his mantle over the younger man's shoulders. The Bible indicates that Elisha arose and followed Elijah, and became his servant (1 Kings 19:21).

Again, this sounds like training to me. I know it was training because when Elijah was taken, Elisha worked twice as many miracles as Elijah did. In order for Elisha to be what he was, he needed to be trained and to have a double portion of Elijah's spirit.

I could have written about some others, i.e., David and Solomon, Paul and Timothy, even Jesus and his disciples. Hey, pastors, we need training. There is nothing wrong with allowing ourselves to embrace pastoral training. I personally feel that training has helped my ministry most. Without the training that I have received, I would have been extremely deficient as a pastor. Most importantly, the people I serve would have received less than God's best. I would encourage you to apply yourself to training in all areas of the ministry.

When we are trained, we can properly train our people to be successful at witnessing and bringing in souls to the Kingdom of God.

While investigating training for myself, I overheard another pastor being mentored by an older pastor. The older pastor was critiquing the younger pastor's Bible class. After listening to one of his tapes, the older pastor told him he was talking about the Word but he was not really teaching the Word. It was then that I discovered I had been doing the same thing, talking about the Word but not really teaching the Word.

Since I've changed the way I teach, my Bible class nights have become like Sunday morning. Some weeks, we are more packed during Bible class than we are on Sunday morning. Simply learning how to properly teach has been a blessing to my ministry.

I could tell you many other training points that have helped me in ministry and caused our church to advance to another level; however, that's not my focus. I'm simply trying to stress the importance of training. I encourage every pastor to apply themselves to training.

Now, let's look at another misconception that young pastors make.

5. If I had a bigger church, then more people would come to the church.

There is a misconception as it relates to the size of the building. Some leaders are under the impression that if they had a larger building, then they would have more people in church. This is not true. I know of plenty of churches that have large buildings but the membership never expands.

The real truth of the matter is if you cannot affect ministry in a small building, you surely will not be able to affect ministry in a larger building. The goal of every pastor should be to fill up the building. Large or small, we should ever be expanding for the Kingdom of God.

In Luke 14:23, Jesus says, "And the Lord said unto the servant, Go out into the highways and hedges, and compel them to come in, that my house may be filled."

Again, God wants his house full. Ministry of the Gospel of Jesus Christ will attract people to the church, and vision will keep them there. A leader's most powerful weapon is his or her vision. Your faithfulness now is the barometer that God considers for promotion in your future.

> Thou has been faithful over a few things, I will make thee ruler
> over many things. (Matt. 25:23)

Learn to be faithful right where God has you. Do not allow yourself to get traumatized just because you only have a few people now. Do your part and be faithful. Don't try to wait until you get more members. No, whatever you would have done if you had a larger membership, start doing those things now. These action steps will count as faith in the eyes of God. Remember, faith without works is dead.

I remember when we first got started. Right away, I went to an accountant to find out what my fiscal obligations were. At that time, we could not even afford the accountant. However, I was looking at our future. God gave us favor with the accountant, and she allowed us to pay her fifty dollars a month. As of today, that accountant is still with us and has watched us grow over the years.

This is just one example of not allowing the size of your church building nor the size of your membership to control your thoughts as it pertains to church operations.

Before I close this section, I would like to tell you one other thing that God led me to do. Early on, God led me to purchase a church software for housing all of our financial records. From the natural, we really did not need it. Trust me, if your Sunday morning offering is less than fifty dollars, you will look at that and say, "Who needs software to keep up with this?"

Well, I obeyed God and purchased the software. That software enabled us to keep up with every dime that came into the ministry. It also helped us keep up with every dime that went out of the ministry. It gave us crisp reports and enabled us to chart our growth from year to year. As a result of proper bookkeeping, we were able to purchase eight thousand square feet of land, only having been a church for just one year. Normally banks require two years of banking information before they will even consider you. However, we were on point with every dime, and it was impressive to the bank.

This software also helped us track attendance and visitor records. Staying on top of inviting people and keeping in contact with visitors who attended our services was extremely important. Having your paperwork in order is important and sets the stage for trust among your current members. Now, let's look at some other aspects of ministry impact that are important in small buildings.

If you are going to have maximum impact, you must make sure you are feeding the right food. What you minister makes a difference. People love to hear about Daniel in the lion's den; however, this is not going to help them from week to week. Please don't get overspiritual on me as if I'm trying to denounce the Bible stories. That's not true. What I'm simply trying to emphasize is people need more real-life, day-to-day issues to be dealt with. After all, they don't have to get into the lion's den. In Daniel's generation and even those immediately following his time, this was very powerful food. Let's realize we are living in a different day.

One of my personal Bible interests is the study of the end-time. I can remember launching a series about end prophecy. I studied this thing completely. I was excited and ready to teach. I just knew that everyone would be just as excited as I was about the new series. Well, when the day came to teach the series, only about three people showed up. I was heartbroken because I could not understand why people were not interested as I was.

The normal approach to a situation like this was to preach one of those good old hell, fire, and brimstone messages for the people who did not show up, letting them know the devil had tricked them out of the Bible class. Personally, I felt they should have been there because, after all, I was only trying to help them.

Well, before I could preach my hell, fire, and brimstone message, God began to deal with my heart. God helped me to realize that the people I was ministering to were not having problems with the end-times. They were having problems with paying their rent, communicating in their marriages, and overcoming discouragement. Although the end-time was great information, it just did not minister to their current needs. God wanted me to minister through his Word to the current needs of his people. What an impact lesson for any teacher to learn. Well, immediately I changed. I put the hell, fire, and brimstone message on the shelf and preached a message of love and concern. God really helped me understand and know this.

If you are going to have true impact in ministry, stay away from ministry that does not minister to people's needs. You will be the only one who benefits from this type of ministry. Keep it simple and spirit filled. Keep it about life and living so that people can touch it, identify with it, and tell others without getting confused. Remember, you may like the Dead Sea scrolls; however, it does not help the congregation. I don't care how anointed you become or how well informed your information is. When your people get home, they will soon forget about the Dead Sea scrolls because those bills coming into the house will refocus their thinking. On the other hand, if you help them to understand what the Lord requires us to do with our money, they will be more inclined to come back because you are ministering to their needs.

Regardless of the size of the building, you need effective ministry in order to have impact. We live in a very competitive religious day. The TV ministries are really being effective, and our people are listening to them and learning.

—

We must stay ahead of what's going on and become wise in the things of God.

Look at the number of churches all around us. Let's face it, there are churches better than yours that your members could attend. With that in mind, take your ministry seriously and appreciate the people who have partnered with you. Truly, it is not the size of the church, it's the impact of the ministry. If ministry impact is low in a small facility, it will still be low even if you moved to a larger facility.

Having impact deals with more than just your preaching and teaching. It deals with your overall organization and management of your church. Don't just pray for impact; put your actions on the line and do what you need to do in order to have impact.

There are many more misconceptions that I have not addressed in this book. However, I tried to hit some of the most frequently heard misconceptions. You can now examine yourself to see what is holding you from your greatness. Next, we are going to look at your church's agenda.

Establishing the Church's Agenda

In my studies on church growth, I've discovered what works for one may not work for all. However, in principle, principles will work for all. Good principles will work in every church regardless of who is working them. That's important to understand. What I'm about to share with you are just good principles. It will require you to work harder and be more dedicated, but the outcome is typically the same . . . increase!

Some churches call it mission statements, slogans, or themes. I like to call it an agenda because it keeps things simple. Every church should have an agenda. Agendas are important because they state the cause of my doing. Why am I doing what I do? An agenda will tell me that. Jesus had an agenda:

> For the Son of Man is come to seek and to save that which was lost. (Luke 19:10)

Personally, I feel this should be the agenda of every church, which means everything you do should be in line with or promotion of your agenda. For the sake of our discussion, let us call this agenda "reaching the lost." If that's truly the agenda, then the pastor must first have actions associated with this agenda.

For example, I like to spend hours in study and prayer each week. This is important if I'm going to reach the lost. The Bible calls us workmen.

> Study to shew thyself approved unto God, a workman that needeth not be ashamed, rightly dividing the word of truth. (2 Tim. 2:15)

When the lost comes to the church, I need to have something of value to say to them. Jesus wants us to minister to people. People need to be ministered to, not with just cute sermons that make the preacher feel good. If you are going to be effective in ministry, you've got to have something to say. Your personal prayer and study time must be of the utmost importance as your agenda is calling for it.

If I were to ask most pastors, especially those who are just getting started, "What is the purpose of your Sunday morning services?" they would not truly understand how to answer. I was asked this question during my training. When I was first asked, I was stuck. I felt it was just necessary to have church and edify the saints. I was also asked what was the purpose of my midweek Bible study. Again, I was stuck. I thought it was for the purpose of condemning and correcting the saints.

Well, I learned that Bible study was to equip the saints for witnessing and being a light in the world. The saints were supposed to go out and invite people to church for Sunday morning. Then Sunday morning was Gospel time, a time for people to hear the Gospel of Jesus Christ and, ultimately, be converted. It's not just a gathering to praise God. I hear so many churches make the mistake of saying "Come on out, we are going to praise God." Well, praising God is part of church, but it is not the agenda. The agenda should be let us be sure to bring someone out, then we will praise God for the salvation of the lost.

> Likewise, I say unto you, there is joy in the presence of the angels
> of God over one sinner that repenteth. (Luke 15:10)

The Bible lets us know that the angels rejoice over one sinner being saved. Consider this: the angels did not rejoice when all the saints came to church. They did not rejoice over how you preached the sermon. They did not rejoice over the praise and worship team. They only rejoiced when one sinner was converted. Can you see this? It all works with the agenda. This is why it becomes so necessary for the pastor to study the Word of God and commit themselves to prayer.

When I first started pastoring, I had to work. However, the more I learned about my responsibilities as pastor, I began to make adjustments. I started setting aside time for more prayer. I was already praying an hour every day. However, I bumped it up to two hours a day.

Additionally, I set aside time to listen to the Word of God. Remember, faith comes by hearing. As pastor, I realized how important it was for me to keep my faith up. I also set aside study time for myself. Not just studying to preach to others, but studying for God to minister to me. This level of dedication will cause God's best to come into your life. You will be saturated with wisdom and understanding beyond the norm. I get excited just thinking about what this has meant to my ministry. I aim, in my heart, to be the best pastor my church can have. I can't account for other churches, neither am I trying to say I'm better than anyone else. However, I will strive to be the best pastor my church can have.

This all falls in line with the agenda and the purpose of the church. Once you have the agenda down, you're now ready to present it to your precious flock. When the flock collectively understands the church's agenda, it becomes very easy to make changes or fix things that are broken. Please be reminded all new pastors must have faith. You might not receive the support from others that you are looking for. In most cases, it's good for you. This way, when God blesses you, no one can take the credit but God. Look at what the scripture says:

Therefore, my beloved brethren, be ye steadfast, unmoveable, always abounding in the work of the Lord forasmuch as ye know that your labour is not in vain in the Lord. (1 Cor. 15:58)

Teaching Social Responsibility to Members

Now you are ready to begin teaching social responsibility to your membership. Remind the members that it is no accident that God has placed them in your church. Look at the scripture:

But now hath God set the members every one of them in the body, as it hath pleased him. (1 Cor. 12:18)

This tells us that God has set everyone in the body of Christ as it pleased him. In other words, it is God's will for them to be a member of your church. After all, your church is where they landed. Truly it was no accident. Neither is any member in the church just there to be there. I believe they have a part to play and should be involved at all times. Regardless of size and age (excluding babies), they will grow up. The sooner you start working with them, the better off you will be.

You should start by asking your church, When the lost come into our services, what are they seeing? Are they seeing disorder or order? Is there too much walking, talking, playing, singing, etc.? These are all things that need to be looked at. This will give the green light to ask the church to partner with you in establishing church order. God is an orderly god, and we need to be orderly people. You will be amazed at how your church performs when they understand social responsibility.

Social responsibility emphasizes this point, it is not just the pastor's church, it's our church! Therefore, each member should understand that they play a vital role in how it functions. Let's now take a look at some of the functional problems that growing churches have.

For example, if everyone is always late to church, then when visitors come in, they will note that services never start on time. Time is critical in your program. If your church develops this haphazard mentality about what time they should be at church, it gets contagious. Before long, if you intended to start at 7:00 p.m., everyone will arrive at 7:30 p.m. Then if you change the start time to 7:30 p.m., people will start arriving at 8:00 p.m. Where does this stop?

Not to mention the fact that if a visitor did come to church, they would have to suffer waiting for members to arrive. That's horrible in the sight of God. When visitors come, the membership should be there excited and ready to welcome them in. With God's help, I've pushed for excellence in this area. We always start our services on time. The members of our church can tell you how I feel about being late. I simply resist lateness, and I refuse to allow this spirit to rob my church of its integrity. It will totally rob your purpose and give you a bad reputation.

So a great place to start setting things in order is your local church regiment for how your church will function. I teach, train, and promote to all members that they must take social responsibility for their church. I ask for their uncompromised support in three areas.

The first area of support is time. I ask all members to support by sacrificing their time to be faithful in Bible class. I also request the same in Sunday morning services. This holds true for any other services and programs that we may have. Members should know that they are responsible for giving God their time by way of church attendance. Now, I realize that people are going to church on the Internet and even attend service through the television. But that's not what the Word of God tells us to do. I want to examine this passage of scripture found in Hebrews.

> Not forsaking the assembling of ourselves together, as the manner
> of some is; but exhorting one another: and so much the more, as
> ye see the day approaching. (Heb. 10:25)

I like the way this scripture reads in the message Bible Translation; "not avoiding worshiping together as some do but spurring each other on, especially as we see the big day approaching."

This plainly tells us we can't avoid being at church. Most members don't take into consideration how important it is for them to come to church. Don't you realize that God has required you to come? Don't you know the angels rejoiced over you when you got saved? They expected you to be instrumental in causing someone else to get saved.

Let's think about this aspect of ministry in comparison to a job. Even your job will not allow you to keep missing work without proper cause. Neither will they tolerate you being late! Reason being is your individual role affects how a company's corporate role is perceived. If the company is not meeting deadlines in a timely fashion due to attendance of employees, what do you think the company will do? You're right, they will start firing people. Even if they do not fire them, their performance review will not lead to a raise in salary. Companies understand the attendance factor, so they have strict guidelines forcing people to comply. Companies have decided not to leave it up to people because people can be totally unfair. Well, I decided long ago not to treat my job better than I treat my savior.

Even schools have fairly structured guidelines for your attendance. You certainly will not receive an A in most cases if you did not attend class. Many courses require you to do presentations and other in class-type work. How come when it comes to God, members don't understand the importance of them being in church?

As a new pastor, I can remember ever so well studying so hard to prepare Bible class, only to have one or two people attend. This type of behavior from members will break the pastor's heart and give the devil the opportunity to discourage him. If the pastor is not careful, he will find himself saying "What's the use?" This is a trick of the enemy. God wants us to be faithful. I say to any member reading this passage to stop right now and ask God to give you the grace to be faithful in your local church.

We can't avoid the responsibility to be at church. If the church's agenda is truly to win souls, then each member must commit to being faithful. When new souls come into the church, you want them to see order, even if it's only a few people. We must respect the law of unity. The law of unity says "two are better than one" and "a threefold cord is not easily broken" (Eccles. 4:9-12).

Let's face the facts; we are better when we operate together. This phrase can serve as a great unity slogan for your church. "We are better when we operate together."

The next area is service. The pastor should not have to do everything. It must be clearly taught that the church needs faithful men and women that understand the purpose of God. These are the kind of people who will not allow their men or women of God to become drowned, worrying about every little aspect of the ministry. The church will need people to keep the garbage out, vacuum the floors, purchase supplies, and much more. We see a great example of this in Acts, in the sixth chapter:

> Wherefore brethren, look ye out among you seven men of honest report, full of the Holy Ghost and wisdom, whom we may appoint over this business. But we will give ourselves continually to prayer, and to the ministry of the word. (Acts 6:3-4)

This is very important if church growth is going to truly be effective. The man of God must be free to hear from God. Someone must be willing to be responsible for the service areas of the church. I remember someone told me that one church hired an outside staffing agency to come in and pass out flyers for their church. It was not because they did not have members, it was because the pastor could not get anyone interested enough in church growth.

It's sad to say, but some members think it is the pastor's job to do everything. They expect him to fast, pray, preach, teach, pass out flyers, and sometimes cook chicken. However, that's not the pastor's job. Do not rob your pastor of his effectiveness, making him operate outside of his call. It will hinder your church. If members truly love their church, then they will have the heart of God in this area.

When I first started Faith Cathedral Church, we were in a community center. I used to have to get to the center early to let down the chairs and set up all of the equipment. Many times, my wife and I had to sweep the floor, pick up paper, etc. By the time people arrived, it appeared that the place was already set up. Bear in mind we set it up, because starting off, we just did not have people to do it. On top of all of this, many times we had to pick people up for church and then drop them off after church. Starting off, we understood that if we did not pick them up, they would not be at church. When I think of this now, I laugh.

When service was over, I had more help. There were others there who helped out tremendously, and as always, I am forever grateful. Even then, people got tired. It was told to me that one person said they did not want to come back because they did not want to help out with the breakdown after the service. Yes, starting out was hard. My wife and I and a few others had a service mentality.

> But ye shall not be so; but he that is greatest among you, let him be as the younger; and he that is chief, as he that doth serve. (Luke 22:26)

We did what we had to do until God made a way for us. The members should be ready to serve the flock of God. Not for prestige or fame, money or notoriety, but for the love and the cause of Christ. Please remember what the word says.

> God is not unrighteous to forget your work and labour of love, which you have showed toward His name, in that you have Ministered to the Saints, and do Minister. (Heb. 6:10)

Everyone must be determined to serve. Everyone must be determined to do his or her part.

Before I move from this section, I would like to share this. I did not have an office while we were at the community center. So I found a restaurant nearby called Tasty Dog. It was there that I would sit and study. It was located near a local school, and students would come in and see me with my Bible and other books, studying. However, that did not move me at all. While I sat there, I can remember thanking God for my new office. I would leave the restaurant on my way to Bible class, early enough to set up. Again, I did not have help at that time, but God gave me grace. Many times, I did not have help afterward, depending on who came to church.

Now, I wanted to put this in the book so that members can understand the role that they play in church growth. Although I was effective, I could have been even more effective if I just had help. Thank God he has rewarded our faithfulness now. Now we have help. Enough help that I can now sit down and write books for the ministering to and encouraging of others.

The last area of responsibility I want to discuss is financial support. Financial support is very important, and each member must be taught the principles of giving. For years, I thought I was a giver. Partly because, I paid my tithes and gave offerings weekly. I truly tried to support my former church the best that I could at that time. However, I had never really been taught why we give and what to truly expect after I give. Neither had I been taught how to use my faith in giving. Please understand I was taught to give my tithe and offering, but that was the extent of it.

When I started pastoring, these were the things I had to learn through training. Here I am again, talking about training. But it is so truly necessary. Once I learned, I was able to teach the membership how to give. One thing that I have learned now serving within a smaller church is we had to learn to embrace giving beyond the norm. We had to give beyond the norm because our goals were big. We wanted to function without strain or struggle. Neither did I ever want to be in a position where we had to hold a service just to make money. I did not want that on my résumé. I truly wanted to practice the principles directly from God's Word in this area. According to how I've been trained, giving must be from the heart. Let's look at a scripture.

> Every man according as he purposeth in his heart, so let him give; not grudgingly, or of necessity: for God loveth a cheerful giver. (2 Cor. 9:7)

Here is what I've learned and what I now teach. Each member has to purpose in their hearts how they are going to give. Then they must not give grudgingly. What really caught my eye was "God loves a cheerful giver." Notice the word *loveth*; it means God continues to love. When I discovered that God loves a cheerful giver, it changed my life and the lives of many of my members.

I could almost write an entire book on this one issue (giving) and how important it is for financial success. Many parishioners are wondering why God won't bless them or why God won't solve their problems. I always like to ask, "What kind of giver are you? Even if you give, how are you giving? Is it just to be seen or is it truly flowing from the heart?"

While growing a church from the ground up, your membership will need to partner with you in meeting the budget needs of your church. Remember, with everything that you do within your church, there will be a cost. From the tissue to the fans, expect to pay some money for these things.

Please allow me to elaborate further about the giving issue. Look at what the Word of God says:

> Bring ye all the tithes into the storehouse, that there may be meat in my House, and prove Me now herewith, saith the Lord of Hosts. If I will not open you the windows of Heaven, and pour you out a blessing, that there shall not be room enough to receive it. (Mal. 3:10)

Now let's look at this same scripture in the message Bible:

> Bring your full tithe to the Temple treasury so there will be ample provisions in my Temple. Test me in this and see if I don't open up heaven itself to you and poor out blessing beyond your wildest dreams.

God tells Israel to bring the money in and then test him to see if he would do what he said he would do. The message Bible goes on to talk about God's part in the process. God says, "I will defend you against marauders, protect your wheat fields and vegetable gardens against plunderers."

You've got to understand it is a blessing to accept the responsibility to provide for the house of God. Everyone should be paying tithes if they are members. In fact, I would encourage every pastor not to allow people who don't pay tithes to hold offices in your local congregation. These people operate outside of scriptural principle and will hijack the future of the next generation. Remember, when we make God's business important to us, he will make our business important to him. In Malachi, God accused an entire nation of robbing him. This is unbelievable in thought, to be accused of robbing God, the person who allows me to live. Well, the reality of the issue is people will shout, speak in tongues, work in high positions in the church, and still rob God. This is why teaching in the area of financial responsibility is so important. At one point, I was like most pastors, afraid to teach on such a sensitive subject. It is certainly understandable, because you never want to be accused of just being money hungry. However, we must seek God for wisdom and have a healthy balance in this area. The real truth is we must teach fiscal responsibility to our members.

Let's look at our enemy, the devil. His program will be funded. During this past recession, I did not see one cigarette company lay off anyone. Neither did I see any of the liquor companies lay off anyone. Satan is going to make sure that drinking and smoking are supported. People who have these habits are going to make sure they get what they need. I heard recently that you could buy individual cigarettes if you cannot afford an entire box.

Look at the cable TV and the pornography industry; they have not skipped a beat. In the middle of the recession, these companies are having unbelievable profits. It's amazing how the evil things of our world have no trouble making it. The drug dealers are still on the streets, functioning without strain or struggle. But God's church is suffering month to month, trying to make ends meet. Having all kind of services, i.e., conventions, anniversaries, appreciation, usher and nurse services, and the like. I'm truly disturbed when I see churches having services just to make money. I have discovered a higher level of living happens when I increase my level of giving.

About two years ago, I stopped collecting offerings after Sunday school. I did so because the members were meeting the budget every week. As long as the budget was being met, there was no need to continue collecting more offerings. Some might say I should have continued and just have more money. On the other hand, whenever we needed more, we simply can ask, and the people have a mind to give.

Some churches collect an offering for everything. You can't have a prayer meeting or a choir rehearsal without collecting an offering. Now I'm not being critical for those that do, I'm simply saying I found a better way. While your church is just starting out, an offering program would do you good. God does not want his church in the red. He wants his church to be able to do great things.

Let me call your attention to another scripture found in Luke 16:10-11.

> He that is faithful in that is least is faithful also in much: and he that is unjust in the least is unjust also in much. If therefore ye have not been faithful in the unrighteous mammon, who will commit to your trust the true riches? And if ye have not been faithful in that which is another man's, who shall give you that which is your own?

Please pay great attention to the words *true riches*. This lets us know that there are spiritual riches that can be entrusted to us. However, we must be faithful with how we handle our money or *unrighteous mammon*, as Jesus calls it. If we are not faithful with our money, how can God trust us with other things?

Many Christian people wonder why they are not receiving the blessings promised in scripture. I would highly encourage everyone to examine the level of his or her hearts in giving. The members must learn to go beyond the norm in giving. When your giving is beyond the norm, then your living is beyond the norm. We must be cheerful givers, ready to obey God from the heart.

Before I leave this area of service, I would like to talk about pastoral giving. Every growing church should have a plan to grow to the point where the pastor can work full-time in ministry. I realize that in our society, growing churches will most often have problems with supporting their pastors full-time. However, this should not be, because the pastor will be far more effective when he or she has time to spend with God. The pastor will have time to develop and get the necessary training needed to give his best service to the church. He will also have more time available to him to meet with God.

Not only will it be a benefit to the church, it will be of great benefit to those who give in the life of their leader. Let's look at another scripture supporting this cause:

> For the scripture saith, Thou shalt not muzzle the ox that treadeth out the corn. And, The labourer is worthy of his reward. (1 Tim. 5:18)

Here is how this same scripture reads in the message Bible:

> Give a bonus to leaders who do a good job, especially that ones who work hard at preaching and teaching.

Scripture tells us, "Don't muzzle a working ox" and "A worker deserves his pay." Please understand that the primary concern is not the ox, it's the people that are being fed as a result of the ox. If the ox can't eat, how can he remain in a healthy condition? So it is with God's pastor. If he or she has to continue to worry how he is going to make ends meet every month, he is not going to be healthy. He will be worn and worried out, giving the adversary opportunity to discourage and cause him to be ineffective in ministry.

Every church must learn to give.

> As the scripture says in Luke 6:38, "Give, and it shall be given unto you, good measure, pressed down, and shaken together, and running over, shall men give into your bosom. For with the same measure that ye mete withal it shall be measured to you again."

I encourage you now to gather your group together and discuss these issues with them. Allowing them to partner with you and setting a clear path for responsibility will be the key to great church growth.

Developing a Team Mentality

Now, I would like to discuss your maturity level as a pastor. This truly means a lot. Now before you get offended, please consider what I'm about to say. We must all grow in the area of our maturity. Consider the words of the Hebrew writer:

> For when for the time you ought to be teachers, you have need that one teach you again which be the first principles of the Oracles of God; and are become such as have need of milk, and not of strong

meat. For every one who uses milk is unskilled in the Word of Righteousness: for he is a babe. But strong meat belongs to them who are of full age, even those who by reason of use have their senses exercised to discern both good and evil. (Heb. 5:12-14)

This passage refers to the fact that a person desiring to pastor has been saved long enough to be mature in the Word. However, you can be mature in the Word but absolutely have no people skills. Certainly, you will have to work with your people not only in spiritual matters, but also in carnal matters of business.

For example, there are people in my church who are able to do things in certain areas better than I can. We have a deacon that's very good with his hands. When it comes to fixing pipes or working with cars, he truly can outclass me. Therefore, I have no problems taking his advice in these areas. Now, this is just one example to help you understand my point. It takes nothing away from who I am as the pastor to allow others to play a role in helping me.

Having self-security as a leader is extremely important. I caution you not to be so focused on your being the pastor that you are unwilling to accept suggestions and input from people who love and desire to help you. God will give you people for every step of your vision. You must be extremely careful that you do all you can to let your people know that you value their input. Even if you don't always live by what they say, let them know you appreciate the help.

Potentially, you will encounter people who are not mature, who will look to cause confusion. These kinds of people need to be called on the carpet early. If left unchecked, they will poison some of the other team members. Unfortunately, they believe that they are always a step ahead of you and, in many cases, will look for opportunities to show you up.

You must ask God, as Solomon did, to give you the wisdom and balance to look beyond these types of people and keep them reasonably in order. Ultimately, the goal is to grow them into maturity and win them as part of the vision.

You must be a good listener, as God will oftentimes speak through those right around you. I cannot tell you the many times that God has used team members directly in our group to speak a word of advice or to give a workable idea. Whether you have two or three team members, take advantage of their ideas. Please understand that God placed them there for a reason. This is not the time to battle as to who can be the smartest. Look at the advice Jethro (Moses's father-in-law) gives Moses.

After he saw all that Moses was trying to do by himself, he told Moses to get a team.

> Moreover you shall provide out of all the people able men, such as fear God, men of truth, hating covetousness; and place such over them. (Exod. 18:21)

Wow, this was great advice. You don't see Moses saying, "No one can judge like me." You don't see him saying, "I must be the one to do everything." No, the advice was good, and Moses obeyed. He developed a team mentality and truly made his workload easier.

Growing churches will have a considerable amount of adversity, reason being is the devil does not want it to work. He wants to kill the church before you even get started. Your people need to understand this and work toward maturity and not allow the enemy to come in and tear up what God is trying to establish. Nothing can be so terrible as a Christian misplaced, looking for a new church, all because of a bad understanding.

This reminds me of an incident I had a few years ago. One Sunday morning, a couple arrived at our church, requesting to see me. Of course, I allowed them to come in my office and talk with me. They quickly shared with me that they wanted to join our church. I asked why so quickly, as it appeared very strange that they would come right in even before the service was started good asking to join. As the discussion continued, I found out that they simply had a disagreement with their pastor of thirteen years. It just happened I actually knew their pastor.

I quickly advised them not to leave like that. As a pastor, I knew the awesome pain that comes when members leave, especially when they were not supposed to. I was prepared to do everything I could to mend the relationship between the couple and their pastor. Long story short, the relationship was mended, and they are still in their church. Because God placed them there, they will be far happier than they ever would have been if they had joined our church abruptly. Each member needs to understand that if God placed them there, leaving because of some adversity is not always the best answer.

Now there will be times when people need to leave. In those times, the church will only grow stronger. Neither will the pastor be as hurt because he or she will realize it was for the best. All in all, you must have a team mentality. I can't stress this enough. Teamwork is important, as it will take a tremendous load off you. Remember Jethro's advice to Moses: always allow others to help you. You will be amazed how people perform when they know that their opinions count.

Providing Direction to the Faithful

There will always be people who are just faithful. They make the church an important part of their lives. They support everything that the church does. These are the people who should be trusted, primarily because they are reliable. It may only be one or sometimes two people, depending on the size of your ministry at this time.

Establish monthly meetings to stay up-to-date on issues that may affect the ministry. You will also be able to continue to stir your vision in the hearts of the faithful. Currently, we call our monthly meetings "keeping excellence alive." Truly, that's our purpose for meeting; we desire to keep excellence alive in our ministry. During these meetings, we discuss everything that pertains to keeping excellence alive. From the ushers' duties to broken microphones, everything is open for discussion. Bear in mind that I don't have to fix everything, but at least it's brought to my attention and resolved.

You must continually point your team to the cause of Christ, which is reaching the lost. It is very important that the team understands the impact that the church as a whole is having. Just because they are not preaching or teaching does not mean they do not have impact. For example, I heard visitors say many times how welcome they felt when the usher greeted them.

You will be surprised at how that one greeting can set the tone for a ministry in the hearts of visitors.

A visitor is your most important member because upon conversion, they will serve to energize your ministry and keep the cause of Christ alive in your church. The question becomes "How do we want to handle visitors that come into the church?" This is what makes the team approach so important. When the entire team is working together in evangelism, then treating visitors correctly will be the responsibility of everyone, not just the pastor.

THE VISITOR:
MOST IMPORTANT MEMBER
OF THE CHURCH

Visitors come in many different types. You will have what I like to call suspect visitors. These are visitors who did not really come with a sincere heart to join your church. They may know of someone in your congregation and are only there just as a vote of support. Most times, they will already belong to a church and are not really looking to switch. You want to be nice to these people as you would any other visitor. However, do not spend too much energy on these individuals, as they are only suspects. Individuals who are not looking to join are truly just visiting.

Then you have what I call rejects. Rejects are individuals who come to the church only because they could not work in order at the church they came from. Most times, they have been to multiple churches and are not willing to settle in at any church. It feels good when they initially come; however, soon you will discover their commitment level is low.

I like to use the term "they are unable to be pastored or mentored." Most of the time, they are just looking for a place to fit in. Maybe they could not fit in where they once were. Their key words are "I came to help you." Please believe me, these kinds of people will rarely ever bring the true help that you need. As soon as they encounter undue pressure they did not expect, they will soon hit the road. Although you will not be able to stop them from coming, please do not waste precious outreach energy trying to recruit these kinds of people. Consequently, these people are temporary and will easily be disturbed and move on.

Then you have what I like to call objects. Objects are simply people who come to get in the way. They may be excited when they first visit your church and even possess some talents that the church can use. However, they will only get in the way of the growth of the faithful. Most times, these are experienced people, already saved. Most times, they cannot be discipled at all. If fact, if you are not careful, you will find yourself allowing them to disciple you. They are constantly reaching for positions and trying to get things done without having a proper commitment to the church. Most times, they will block others who are less talented from serving because of their talents. Truly they have the talent, but they lack the commitment for long-term service. In this case, you will be glad when they come and even happier when they leave.

Objects will drain your energy and time. You must understand what type of visitor you are dealing with so that you can detour any efforts to stop your progress. Remember, you always want to make sure you are dealing with people who are called to your work. I've always prayed that God would send people who are called to the assignment he has given me.

Now, please understand that God has people who are called to your ministry. They may have come from another church and have experience that can help your church. When God really plants them, they will walk in great wisdom and will not cause any problems to disrupt the vision of your church. It has been my experience that these people will fit right in. Not only will they fit in, they will do your church good.

The last group I would like to discuss is called prospects. These are the people you want to spend your time trying to help. Prospects are visitors who do not know the Lord Jesus Christ as their savior. Neither are they currently attending any other church. Most times, these are people who a member of your congregation has invited and has probably been witnessing to them already. When we get visitors that meet this description, the congregation, as well as myself, are very excited. This person becomes a great candidate for membership. Remember this, the fact that they have come to the church is a huge indication that God has his drawing hand all over them.

> No man can come to Me, except the Father which has sent Me draw him. (John 6:44)

You will be amazed at how one convert can bless your church. I remember one convert at our church was used by God to bring in others. Once she was converted, she was instrumental in bringing her friend, her coworker, and others. You just never know who God is going to use.

When you are dealing with visitors, it's important to really be able to understand what is good and what is bad in terms of growing your church. I certainly do not want to sound like I'm picking apples; however, you must protect your energy and time. I've learned from experience that the enemy will do everything he can to distract your outreach time. There is no sense fishing for catfish where only perch fish are located. You will waste your time.

You want your members to invite prospects, people you can minister to who have a chance of getting saved and joining your church. Sometimes it is hard to get this type of people into the church, but when you get them, the stage is set for God to move. This is what real evangelism is all about, reaching the unsaved, unchurched, and untaught. It is about working with and inviting the right kind of people. Spending your time in good harvest on ripe soil. No one plants a seed on bad soil; we all know that's a waste of time. Now let's look at what is possible as it relates to church growth, right where you are today.

Keys to Effective Evangelism

1. The Invite

Remember that the goal of the invite is to get them to the church. I realize that coming to church will not change their lives, but once they get to church, the Gospel will. Remember, you must be prepared to preach the Gospel to reach the lost. Being prepared is key, giving God a well-rested, prayed, and studied body.

Members should witness to the individuals about being saved either before or after they attend. Most members make the mistake of trying to preach and save the person right then and there. Most members hit them with a lot of scriptures and discuss with them the sins that they have committed. Now in some instances, this is OK if God has truly led you to do that. However, you will be most successful in church growth just focusing in on the invitation.

We certainly do not promote gimmicks or schemes and want to be forthcoming in our invitation. Most people are impressed by word of mouth. So the first thing your invite should contain is some statement about how the church has been effective in your life. It must be something that people can relate to.

For example, you can tell people God is in that church. When I went there, I had bad credit; but since I've been there, God has totally turned my credit all the way around. Again, this is just one example. Obviously it must be true. I used credit because everyone is not on drugs and alcohol. Or you can talk about how God healed your body. Emphasis is this: you must give them a benefit or show them a benefit that the church has had in your life. Please do not give them a long-drawn-out story. Notice a commercial is only about a minute long. Some commercials are thirty seconds. All you need to do is perfect your commercial for God.

In growing churches, each member needs a commercial. A commercial is a short story that you give people about how your church has been effective in your life. For example, I used to say, "I make far better decisions now." People can relate to things like that. The commercial should be something quick and brief about how the church has helped your life. However, even after we have witnessed to them, we will be more successful inviting people to a cause, not just inviting them to church. You will be amazed at the results.

Now there are several kinds of invitations. I've placed them into categories to make invites extremely easy to follow. The first invite is what I call the conviction invitation. The conviction invitation is when a person sees or has a mighty revelation of God. At that moment, they are so persuaded that they need to come to Christ they cry out, "What must I do?"

Let me now explain what I mean. The conviction invitation is driven by the hand of God, but the invite and directive is provided by the Christian. We can clearly see this in Acts 16:28-31. Paul and Silas were locked in jail wrongfully, and the prison keeper saw the awesome hand of God deliver them and was convicted. Look at the text:

> But Paul cried with a loud voice saying, "Do yourself no harm: for we are all here." Then he called for a light, and sprang in, and came trembling and fell down before Paul and Silas. And brought them out, and said, "Sirs, what must I do to be saved?"

I remember when I was shot at point-blank range. I certainly should have already been dead. But I knew God's hand was upon my life, and I was in awe realizing how he delivered me from the hand of my enemy. My precious aunt took advantage of this moment and invited me to church. Well, I went, and that was a key start to the salvation process in my life. Again, because of what I had just been through, I had a conviction upon me. My aunt took advantage and invited me to church. The emphasis here is taking advantage of the invite when a person has been in a situation where God delivered them.

The next invitation is what I would like to call the opportunity invitation. This invitation takes advantage of a ministry moment. A ministry moment is a moment when a coworker, family member, friend, or someone you just know comes to you for prayer concerning a problem that they are having, or they ask for clarity on a biblical subject. There are times when God will allow people to come to you with either a problem or a question. You must have the wisdom at that opportunity to seize the moment.

Again, God can always lead an individual to say the right thing and win that person to Christ. As a general rule, when people come to you with problems, most times it's effective to just listen. Any psychiatrist will tell you while addressing problems with people, the first thing you should do is listen. Allowing people to talk it out is therapy. Once you have listened to them, then the opportunity will present itself. This is where you now talk about the value of having Christ in your life. This is not the time to talk to them about going to hell. The Gospel is good news. Talk to them about the value of Christ in the lives of people.

The scriptures tells us of such a moment in the life of Philip the Preacher. The Bible says that Philip overheard the man of Ethiopia, a eunuch reading the prophet Isaiah, and asked him, "Do you know what you are reading?"

> And Philip ran thither to him and heard him read the Prophet Isaiah and said, "Do you understand what you are reading?" And he said, "How can I, except some man should guide me?" And he desired Philip that he would come up and sit with him. (Acts 8:30-31)

Sometimes, opportunities like these come from eating lunch at your job, school, etc. You perceive that someone just needs a bit more understanding about the things of God. When the opportunity presents itself, you must react. It serves as a time to love and show concern for others. Again, the Holy Spirit must guide us in our efforts at all times.

The emphasis is making the invitation. I cannot stress this enough! Members must be trained to make the invitation.

Then there is a divine invitation. This is when God divinely places someone in your path to witness to. Most times, these are people you won't even know or have seen before, whether in the store, doctor's office, mall, etc. God divinely places someone in your path just for you to witness and invite them to church. Ultimately, God confirms his hand by saving them and causing them to be fruit that remains. Sometimes God will place people upon your heart. Then he will allow you and that person to cross paths. Divine moments can always be recognized because there is a yearning in your spirit to witness, and God supplies the right words.

This reminds me of the story of Acts 10, where Peter is commissioned to go with the servants from Cornelius's house. God had divinely orchestrated a meeting between Peter and Cornelius.

> There was a certain man in Caesarea called Cornelius, a centurion of the band called the Italian band. A devout man and one who feared God with all his house, which gave much alms to the people and prayed to God always. He saw in a vision evidently about the ninth hour of the day an Angel of God coming in to him and

saying unto him, "Cornelius." And when he looked on him, he was afraid, and said, "What is it Lord?" And he said unto him, "Your prayers and your alms are come up for a memorial before God. And now send men to Joppa and call for one Simon, whose surname is Peter. He lodges with one Simon a tanner, whose house is by the seaside: he shall tell you what you ought to do."

Now the question remains: what do I do when I don't have a conviction invitation to give, neither is there an opportunity invitation or divine invitation to give? This brings us to the next invitation.

The next invitation is called the kingdom invitation. A kingdom invitation is when I just invite someone. You may not know if they are hurting or going through anything; you just invite them. We see Paul in the sixteenth chapter in Acts develop this unique relationship with Timothy. The scripture says as he went to Derbe and Lystra, he saw a disciple by the name of Timothy. Paul took him under his wing and mentored him in the faith. In the thirteenth verse of the same chapter, Paul met a woman named Lydia, a seller of purple of the city of Thyatira, who worshipped God. The Lord opened her heart, and she was converted.

I could go on and on with examples from scripture of kingdom invitations presented in the Bible. We must learn from the example of scripture to make our kingdom invitations at all times. Now let's take a closer look at the kingdom invitation.

THE KINGDOM INVITATION

You can't assume that your members truly know how to invite people to your local church. Therefore, leave nothing to chance; you must train them. Most times when you invite someone to an event, you must be able to share with them how the event is going to be good for them.

For example, if I invite you to my birthday party, I might say, "We are going to have a lot of good food." Or I could say, "Come to my wedding reception. I've reserved a seat for you as my special guest." People love to be invited someplace where there is a welcoming invite with something good in it for them.

So we must train our people to not just invite them to church; anyone can do that. We must learn to invite them to a cause. For example, "Our choir is presenting their first concert tonight and we are trying to invite as many people as we can to come out and join us. Would you be my special guest? I've already arranged special seating just for you."

Here is another example. "Tonight, our bishop is preaching on marriage. He has asked us to invite other married couples we know to come out and be with us. He has even allotted a special gift budget for all of our visitors. I thought about you and your spouse and would like you to be my special guest."

I might add, his teaching on marriage has taught my wife and me how to communicate and has greatly impacted our lives. We hardly ever have an argument because we have been taught the power of proper communication. My point is this: when you invite someone to church, you must have a cause and a benefit associated with the invitation. This makes for a very impactful invitation.

In Matthew 28:36-38, there is an interesting passage of scripture that I believe falls directly in line with the kingdom invitation.

> But when He saw the multitudes, He was moved with compassion on them, because they fainted, and were scattered abroad, as sheep having no shepherd. Then said He unto His disciples, "The harvest truly is plenteous, but the labourers are few. Pray you therefore the Lord of the Harvest, that he will send forth labourers into His Harvest."

Here, Jesus is having a conversation with his disciples, and he tells them a key point. "The harvest truly is plenteous." This one statement alone helps me understand that there is no shortage on people to be saved. Now you must understand the word *plenteous* is a key word. Jesus called it plenteous. The word *plenteous*, according to Webster, comes from the word *plenty*. *Plenty* means I have more than enough. I submit to you that the harvest or, properly related, the "world" has plenty or more then enough people you can invite to church.

Now let me unveil a very simple method that I believe will work for any growing church. Whether you have ten or twenty members, it will work. Before I tell you of this method, please allow me to lay some foundation as to why it works.

The Law of Numbers

In the business world there is a business principle called the law of numbers. People of marketing and business have performed studies, which, I might add, are very consistent. The studies show that if I invite one hundred people to try my product, at worse, I will get a 1 percent return. So out of a hundred, I will get one person to try my product. At a best-case scenario, I will get a 3-5 percent return, or three to five people trying my product. This is why an appeal is made to many people.

Companies invest large amounts of money into blanket advertising with the expectation of a small return. Advertisers know that over time, they will grow on purpose because of blanket marketing. The key point is the businesses have a growth plan.

Now, some people may be offended just to consider having a growth plan in the church. I've heard pastors say things like "I'm waiting on my season," or "I'm just waiting on God." Take note, Jesus did not tell us to do that. He told us that the harvest is truly plenteous, but the laborers are few. I personally don't believe the laborers are few because we have members who could work. However, the laborers are few because God's people don't want to work. Can you see that? The average Christian goes weeks without inviting anyone to church.

Even with this invitation, it's casual and very low-key. No real planned effort goes into the invitation. Every business grows because of a plan or a product in high demand that meets the needs of people. We as God's leaders must develop a plan and purpose that will draw people from the world into the harvest of God. If Jesus tells us to send in labors, then I believe that the laborers' work will not be in vain. Let's look at a scripture concerning the disciples working for the Lord.

> And they went forth, and preached every where, the Lord working with them, and confirming the word with signs following. (Mark 16:20)

Notice what this scripture says: "the Lord working with them." It did not say the Lord working for them. It said the Lord was working with them. In other words, they had to put forth some effort. We can clearly see their effort: "they went forth, and preached every where." This is what they, the disciples, did. They went forth and preached. Emphasis, they did something. They did not sit back and do nothing.

Also notice what the Lord did while working with them. The Lord "confirming the word with signs following." The Lord made sure that he did not leave them helpless; he worked with his laborers, confirming the Word with signs following. That's awesome!

Growth Plan

Now let's talk about a very simple plan that will change your church overnight. Truly, I mean your church can change overnight. Please understand it takes proper administration and teaching to facilitate this type of plan. However, with the right focus and determination, it can be done. Please also remember that you need some fasting and prayer to apply spiritual power to this type of growth plan.

I understand that on average, it takes six visitors before our church is able to pick up a new member. Now please understand this is in general, not law. Certainly there are times when people will visit once, get saved, and join the church. However, on average, it will take at least 6 visitors before you can pick up a new family.

With that in mind, if I wanted to grow my church by one member every month, then I understand I need at least 6 visitors attending my church that month. Let me remind you these visitors should be primarily unchurched, unsaved, and untaught. Remember, these kinds of people are what we call prospects. People you know that do not attend another church. This way, you are not in competition with any other churches. These are the best people to invite. Please understand you can invite others, but unchurched people are the best for new membership.

Now let's look at the numbers because this is important. Remember, the goal is to get one new family every month. This means we need at least 6 members per month. If you can get six unchurched, untaught, unsaved visitors in your church every month, your church will grow.

Considering the law of numbers, 6 visitors represent 1 percent of 600. Just for clarity purposes, 60 people would be 10 percent of 600. Can you see that? So depending on the commitment level of my members, we could chart a very aggressive course of action or a less aggressive course of action. First, let's look at an aggressive course of action.

Let's assume that your church only has 20 adult members or members who have the age and intelligence to be a witness for Jesus Christ. From week to week, you only experience having those 20 members in church every Sunday.

You have been praying to God for more members, and it appears things are hopeless. You and your church should try to work this plan prayerfully and with proper teaching.

In order to get 6 visitors on a monthly basis, your invitation goal should be to invite 600 unchurched, untaught, unsaved visitors on a monthly basis. Believe me, I understand that it can be difficult to invite 600 people in one month. However, when you break it down, it becomes very easy to accomplish. With 20 adult members, each member should be responsible for inviting at least 30 visitors a month. This breaks down to 7.5 visitors being invited on a weekly basis by each member. How long would it take to go out and witness to approximately 8 unsaved, unchurched, and untaught visitors? I'm confident it would only take thirty minutes to an hour to invite these people to church. Remember, the goal is simply to invite them to church, not to preach to them or solve all of their problems, nor give them a lot of money; just invite them to church.

What would happen if you have 30 adult members? This means that each member would only have to invite twenty prospects a month. Now let's break this down. Each member would have to invite 5 prospects a week. How long would it take for each member to invite 5 prospects a week? You're right, it would not take long at all.

What would happen if you have 50 adult members? This means that each member would only have to invite 12 prospects a month. This breaks down to three people every week. How long would it take you to invite 3 people to your church on a weekly basis? By now, you get my point. The more people you have, the easier the process gets. This is evangelism at its basic level, simply making sure someone is being invited to the church on a weekly basis.

Now let's look back at the twenty members. Let's say that only ten of the members took evangelism to heart and the other ten failed miserably and did not do anything. Considering this, this still means you are inviting three hundred people to your church on a monthly basis and seventy-five prospects on a weekly basis. I'm confident that's more people being invited to your church than you presently are inviting. Because most churches, especially smaller growing churches, are not inviting enough people to church. Many times, they make the mistake of inviting the same people to church over and over. This is a mistake. I understand that you should invite people over and over; however, don't get stuck on them. Invite other prospects because the Lord will work with you, "confirming his word with signs following."

What you will do is create a sturdy stream of new unchurched, unsaved, untaught prospects into your church on a monthly basis. I've tracked our visitors every year. On average, we have approximately two visitors every week. If you are starting a church from the ground up, you must have a sturdy stream of visitors coming into your church at all times. Now you position yourself to grow on purpose, not by happenstance. With two to four visitors attending your services every week, by the end of the year, you should have grown your church by at least three to five families.

Now if you add some prayer and fasting to this plan, there is no telling what God will do. God is the only one that can give increase. Understand when we do our part, then God is obligated to work with us. We've looked at these numbers from a 1 percent return. I wonder what would happen if God gave us a 3 percent return. Wow, that would be some kind of growth.

The key emphasis is your church can have a simple plan that laborers can understand and use. The use of the plan gives God an works seed, and God is obligated to bless your harvest. Remember, invite people to a cause, not just to church. So the church must have cause-driving services and not just service. You will often hear announcements coming from the pulpits of many churches, saying, "This is family and friends Sunday." Again, this is just a way to give people a cause to come to church. Other churches have healing services or salvation services. Whatever the cause is, be prepared to invite people to church.

Conversion Growth Rate

I'm a firm believer that every pastor starting a church from the ground up should look at his church's conversion growth rate within his church. Conversion is simply tracking how many visitors you had this year and how many of them were converted. Let's look at a simple example.

If you had 20 prospect visitors in a year's time, out of the 20, how many of them were converted? Remember, you want to track the right prospects. Only track those that are untaught, unchurched, and unsaved. You should be able to easily get this information from the people who invited them. Let's say, for example, out of the 20 prospect visitors, 2 of them were converted. This gives your church a 10 percent conversion rate. That's great for any church. Having a 10 percent conversation rate is a powerful thing, and this is exactly where you would like to be.

Now let's say out of the 20 prospect visitors, only 1 was converted. That gives you a 5 percent conversion rate, and again, that's great; however, it only represents a 5 percent conversion growth rate. This simply identifies the work that must be done in your church. It gives us faith goals to shoot for in the upcoming year.

With this information, every pastor can judge the conversion rate of their church and then begin to employ methods to improve it. You should get the members involved on helping them understand your church's conversion growth rate. I truly believe that the members of your congregation desire to be in a healthy situation. Equipped with information, you can get the entire membership involved in church growth.

Establishing Faith Goals

Every year, we establish faith goals for our church in every area. A faith goal is simply a planned achievement that you are standing in faith for God to grant. You should set a faith goal for financial increase, membership increase, and internal growth increase. Regardless of the area, the key point is having a faith goal. I'm a firm believer that you must plan, prepare, and pray for increase with your church.

You should share your financial, membership, and internal growth goals with your members. Then introduce them to a faith plan of action to achieve the goals you are believing God for. For clarity purposes, I would like to give you an example of faith goals.

Our financial faith goal next year will be to average $10,000 in church income every month. We will do this by increasing our current tithe and offerings from 62 percent of everyone paying tithes to 82 percent of people paying tithes. Again this is just an example of a church faith goal.

I would like to give you another example, as it relates to membership. Our church faith membership goal is we will increase our membership this year by ten families. We will do this by launching four outreach campaigns for the upcoming year. Our campaigns are designed to launch invite initiatives for the unchurched, untaught, and unsaved. Now bear in mind that this is only one way to work church growth, not the only way. Be sure to empower your membership with invite cards or flyers, equipping them with what they need to begin to invite people to the church.

I remember working this same principle within my congregation. At the time, we only had about fifteen real faithful adults. I asked each one to think of three people that they could invite. Over about a four-week period, we worked on our cause and our invitation cards. Well, it worked; on the day of the service, we had about fifteen visitors in addition to our normal crowd. Now to some, this seems to be not much at all, but to those starting from the ground up, this was huge. We were simply not used to this kind of a crowd.

Again, everyone was not successful, and as you can suspect, every visitor invited did not come. We had approximately forty-five solid invites to unchurched, untaught, and unsaved people. Well, fifteen of the visitors invited attended the service. Of course, we prayed and fasted to add additional spiritual pressure on our harvest. I'm proud to say that some of these visitors are now members, filled with the Spirit of God, and are a great blessing to our church.

Please understand there are churches that grow at an unbelievable rate. I call these types of churches exceptions to the rule. Sometimes they grow because of some celebrity status their pastor has attained. Some churches have pastors who are simply great preachers, which cause their churches to grow. However, as soon as the preacher dies or can't preach anymore, the members are gone. Some churches grow exceptionally well, strictly by God's divine providence for that city or area. Long story short, it's very difficult to diagnose church growth. For some, it's simple; for others, it involves diligence. Again, churches that grow at unbelievable rates are exceptions and not the norm. I believe we can learn from exceptional growth situations and try to understand what is causing people to flock to the church in great numbers.

Churches who do not experience exceptional growth situations must learn not to be discouraged because God will reward our faith on any level when properly applied, keeping in mind that the goal is to get people to come and try your church out. Any new restaurant wants everyone to come and try out what they are cooking. We should desire the same thing. At most restaurants, if people like the service and food, they come back. So it is with churches; if people like the service and the food, they come back. Well, we understand that this is not all together like a restaurant. I am simply trying to state that we must do our part to be faithful and diligent regarding new souls entering our church.

Before we conclude this section, please understand there is no substitute for praying and fasting. Praying and fasting adds the spiritual pressure that's so necessary for soul-winning campaigns. This reminds me of a scripture found in Psalms:

> Except the Lord build the house, they labour in vain that build it: except the Lord keep the city, the watchman waketh but in vain. (Ps. 127:1)

Regardless of what we do, we must keep God at the forefront of our efforts. God is the one that will provide the increase to our harvest. Now before we get into other church growth ideas, let's take a look at services.

SERVICES

Let's take some time to discuss services. Your services must be designed and driven with your visitors in mind. There was once a time we could get away with having a four-hour service easily. Some churches have even gone longer than that. Please realize that a very long service is an automatic turnoff to visitors. We might like it because we have been converted and understand the goodness of God. We may even have a sincere desire to minister in song, preaching, etc. However, in this generation, this will turn most visitors, especially the unchurched, completely off. Now notice, I said most visitors. Not everyone will be turned off, especially if God has truly sent someone to your church to be planted. However, this may not happen every week, so I think we should plan with our visitors in mind.

Most people want to get to the Word. Yes, they may like the singing, but trust me, they are more into what the pastor is going to preach about. I attribute this to the technology age that we are living in. Things are quick and moving, getting directly to the point of the matter. This is what most unchurched people will first look for.

I believe Sunday morning service should only last an hour and a half to two hours at the most. Again, this is just my observation and opinion. Holding long services will cause a visitor to focus on how long they have been at church. Please understand the devil is going to make sure this is their focus. When it is time for the ministry of the Word, the visitor is already distracted and turned off. This is a tragedy and should not happen in any service. Now, we understand that God will divinely take over some services, and they will automatically go longer. In those times, we are totally out of control and render all control to the ministry of the Holy Spirit.

You should consider the time to preach and make sure you leave time for the altar call. This is so very important. If the visitors are thinking, *I have to leave*, they will not even consider the altar call, which, in my opinion, is the most important part of the service. Let's look at the scripture on this point:

> Likewise, I say unto you, there is joy in the presence of the angels
> of God over one sinner that repenteth. (Luke 15:10)

Can you see that? The angels did not rejoice over the service, neither did your preaching impress God. However, when one sinner gets up and says "I want to be saved," then all of heaven is at attention. I'm always excited when someone comes forth from the altar call, saying, "I want to be saved" because I understand right then, the angels are rejoicing when one sinner repents. This is what the cause of Christ is all about, sinners.

Keep in mind that people can only sit so long. Yes, you might have older or elderly people who do not mind sitting and being in church longer. They must be made to understand the church is on assignment to save souls. Our services are designed to reach the lost. While we are targeting visitors for the conversion experience, we need the understanding of all members, young and old. Monitoring our time in singing, testifying, praying, etc., is extremely important. Praying for God to speak through your pastor is a must every week.

Timeliness

Let's take some time to discuss services in greater detail. Some growing churches are plagued with people who don't come to church on time. These same people go everywhere else on time. They go to their jobs on time, their schools on time, the dentist's appointment on time, and personal business appointments on time. God's church is the only place that suffers from late saints. Therefore, the church ends up waiting on the bulk of the people to get to the church before they start services. This is a great mistake. You must always be on time for God and hold his service schedules with the utmost integrity. After all, you just never know who is coming to church.

Again, this points to membership taking social responsibility for their church. I would ask the members a simple question: is this how our church is truly going to function? Let them answer the question. This late issue is a direct reflection of the hearts of the membership as to how their church will function. I can only imagine how God feels about our haphazard, lazy attitude about getting to church on time. Let's look at a scripture concerning faithfulness:

> Who then is a faithful and wise servant, whom his lord hath made ruler over his household, to give them meat in due season? Blessed is that servant, whom his lord when he cometh shall find so doing. Verily I say unto you, That he shall make him ruler over all his goods. (Matt. 24:45-47)

Notice the emphasis words *faithful and wise servant*, because this is the one who the Lord has made ruler over his household. If lateness is plaguing your church, it is time for an urgent meeting to help your members understand how much their tardiness hurts. It really hurts when it is consistent and all the time.

Now I understand that we do have our moments when things just don't go right, especially on Sunday morning. I also know that Sunday morning is a spiritual time, and the god of this world, Satan, knows this. He works in the hearts of people just to make them late for church. If you are not careful, everyone, from the ushers to the musicians, will be late getting to church. Then your service begins to look like some gong show that just came together at the last minute. It does not look like a purposefully planned service where people's hearts are ready to receive what God is saying that morning.

Satan will use late members to frustrate the pastor, especially new pastors who have not learned the tricks of the adversary to throw him or her off their assignment for the day. If you as a pastor are not careful, you will find yourself preaching something totally contrary to what God had in mind.

Lateness in church will also weaken other members and cause them to accept lateness as the norm. People are impacted by seeing what other people have done or are doing. For example, if the primary president over an auxiliary is late, then it becomes easy for the members of that auxiliary to look at the president and say in their hearts, "If they can do it, I will too." This is why the people who are put out front are so important, because they write a mental experience for everyone else as to what is acceptable and unacceptable.

Could you imagine if 50 percent of your church was late for church all the time? This would be tragic for any congregation. Now I've come to the conclusion that all churches will have late people, but this should be heavily monitored to keep your church on track.

Let's examine for a moment the standards that most jobs establish. I used to work for Arthur Andersen. This was a great company to work for until it was closed down. At one point, the employees would punch in at a time clock, noting the time that they arrived. Then those punch cards were given to payroll for personnel. If a person was late twice, it was a write-up. If they were late more than twice many times, their jobs were threatened. Can you see this? The world understands the importance of having timely employees; what about the church? Every member has the responsibility to uphold his or her service times at all times.

Sometimes churches are plagued with musicians that show up any time they want to. The pastor is scared to tell the musician that his behavior is not appreciated for fear of losing them. Please understand you are going to eventually lose them anyway, because if they do not have respect for God and his program, neither will they have respect for you. The slightest bit of pressure will run them away.

Pastor, you are responsible for setting the guidelines for respect and what is tolerable in your church. A church without proper guidelines will soon be haphazard and lose the true meaning of fulfilling their assignment. Since musicians play a vital role in the music area, it is very important that clear guidelines be established up front. Once guidelines are agreed upon, each party has a responsibility to uphold their end of the agreement. Establishing written guidelines for musicians will prove very helpful to your church.

Opening of the Service

The opening of the service is important, especially in smaller growing churches. I am a firm believer that this is a key time of the service. It is the time to let the devil know we are on assignment for God. Opening the service is the time when all members should become ministry minded. It makes no difference what happened at home before you got to church. When the opening of the service starts, it is time to worship God.

This is why I like to open the services up with prayer. We used to open up with singing. However, I found out that opening the service up with prayer, making everyone stand and getting each person involved, sets the tone for the entire service. With the opening prayer, you need someone that loves to pray and is anointed to pray. You need someone who can engage God's Spirit early on in the service. Now this is what works for us. I realize some people have great praise and worship starting the service out. Keep in mind, this is good if it works for you. My only point is this: getting off to a great start is important.

One of the things that I learned while playing high school basketball was the value and importance of getting the team off to a good start. It always appeared when we got off to a good start, we were always in for a strong finish. My coach at the time would try to get me easy shots early in the game. He realized the game would flow better for me once I had made a couple of baskets early.

On the flip side of this, when the basketball team did not get off to a good start, we ended up struggling for most of the game. Almost like climbing up a hill that seemed to be getting taller the farther we climbed. I would like to add: most of those games, we lost.

Even in racing, racers would tell you the importance of them getting off to a good start. Some racers lose the race at the very beginning all because they failed to get off to a good start. In racing, the racers spend hours just practicing getting off the blocks. Over and over, they start and stop, start and stop, trying to set the tone for a great start.

Well, I firmly believe the start of any service is important and should be protected. Getting off to an anointed start in any service helps to set the tone for an anointed finish. We place great emphasis on who starts all of our services.

Pulpit Educate

Now let's take a look at how important it is to watch what is said across the pulpit. This is a very critical part of ministry. In the very beginning of this book, I asked a question as to whether or not you wanted your church to grow. Well, if you do, this section of the book is critical to your attention.

Does the term *perception* mean anything to you? A person's perception is their reality, and when it comes across the pulpit, it is impossible to get it back. Let me give you an example my pastor once gave me. He told me words are like feathers; once they are out, you just can't get them back. For example, a man finds a box of feathers. Unbeknownst to him, his daughter had collected them over time for a science project she is currently working on. He takes the box of feathers onto the roof of the house and tosses them over, and the feathers go everywhere. When the daughter arrives and discovers her feathers are missing, she asked the father, "Where are they, and can I get them back?" Well, you can imagine how difficult it would be to get the feathers back. So it is with words; once you put them out over the pulpit, people will perceive what is being said. Keep in mind, their perception is their reality.

For example, if you say, "The devil is trying to stop our service, I want everyone to get up and shake the devil off," this can be perceived in a negative light. Now the seasoned saint is not offended many times at all. But the visitor will leave, saying, "That lady or man said I had a devil on me." Satan will work overtime to distort any uncalculated words just to turn your prospect off.

I have seen churches in the middle of praise service say, "Turn to your neighbor and say, 'Anything dead needs to be buried.'" Now, in the mind of the visitor, this can be viewed very negatively. Because Satan, your adversary, is going to tell them, "These people are calling you dead." I hope you get my point. The emphasis is simply watching what you say across the pulpit at all times. Let's look at another scripture:

> Neither give place to the devil. (Eph. 4:27)

This scripture tells us to give no place to the devil. In other words, we should not give the devil anything negative to work with in our words.

Some churches still have testimony service. I have heard some of the most terrible testimonies, and I have heard some of the funniest testimonies. I have also heard some very good testimonies that truly influence and encourage people in positive ways. Whatever your preference is, please train your people how to give good testimonies that glorify God. Testimonies should not be long and drawn out. It makes no difference how big or small the church is. Testimonies should be quick, Jesus focused, with a victorious outcome. Let's look at some examples.

I have heard people get up to testify and say, "I was not coming today because the devil has been really fighting me." Well, what kind of hope does that give to a sinner who is looking for a better life? If the saints do not want to come to church, why should the sinners? You are telling people that the devil is winning in your life. As long as Satan knows he can use you to testify of his great power to discourage people from coming to church, he will use you. That spirit is contagious and will transfer to others within the congregation. If you are not careful, visitors will get the impression that the saints are just as depressed or as worried as they are. I am positively certain that no member or leader desires things like this to happen in their church.

I believe these are times when the devil steals the service. Have you ever been in a service when something was said or done to change the atmosphere? There are times when God is moving in worship, and someone who is not sensitive to the Spirit will sing a song totally out of place. Please understand I do not literally believe the devil can steal a service, but my point is he will fight to disrupt the service. He does it by testimonies that don't glorify God. He also does it when people get in the flesh while trying to minister in song or testimonies, etc.

We must truly be mindful of what we say across the sacred desk. This is where training is so vitally important. Do yourself a favor and train people in your church to be mindful of what is said across the pulpit.

Offerings

This is a very sensitive area within churches, but it is an area that must be talked about and discussed. Sometimes we spend countless hours trying to lift offerings, especially when the church is small and growing. I am a firm believer that offerings should be handled in excellence. The first point of excellence is teaching and training people to give.

People should understand why they give, what they are giving for, and the benefit of the promises that God has promised to supply as a result of their giving. Here is a practice that has truly helped our church. During the course of the year, I have two meetings. In those meetings, I discuss in a high-level overview the financial picture of the church. My aim is to give the congregation a quick glimpse as to what it takes to run our church budget for the year. Once the budget is identified, we know what our Sunday morning financial goal is every Sunday. Then the members are taught to take personal responsibility for doing their part in giving to God.

This must be followed with a biblical teaching on giving principles of the Bible. Teaching what God says about money is important and must be explained in clear, precise detail. When the Word truly gets into the hearts of faithful members, giving will become a part of life. Let's look at a scripture:

> Every man according as he purposeth in his heart, so let him give; not grudgingly, or of necessity: for God loveth a cheerful giver. (2 Cor. 9:7)

This is a great scripture, which I could easily spend five or six pages explaining. However, I want to focus on one thing. Notice the part that says "every man purposeth in his heart so let him give." What a revelation to understand that I have a responsibility, even before I come to church, to purpose in my heart what I am going to give to God. Now if you purpose not to pay your tithe, what do you think God thinks about that? I know this is a tough question, but it is one that every member must answer if they are serious about being blessed by God. If you have come to church with the purpose of heart to rob God, how can you be successful? Let's look at another scripture:

> Will a man rob God? Yet ye have robbed me. But ye say, wherein have we robbed thee? In tithes and offerings. (Mal. 3:8)

In other words, you have robbed me by not purposing in your hearts your responsibility to give. Look at what God actually calls it, rob God. God claims he is being robbed from week to week. People wonder why they are struggling to make ends meet. They are struggling because God is being robbed. Can you see this? I often tell our members that a church cannot be judged on how many people fill the pews, but a church should be judged on the willingness of the hearts of it's members. When members have willing hearts, the church will never go lacking.

Now look at the last part of the first verse that says, "God loves a cheerful giver." I submit to you today that God does not want your gift if you can't give it cheerfully without regret. Think about that, would you want people to give you anything, and while giving it to you, they really do not want to? Well, God feels the same way about you giving to him.

This is just a quick principle that should be taught in every small or growing church. If you are growing a church from the ground up, you're going to need some money. Your members should be able to understand that they will have to give beyond the norm. It is truly in giving when you find out who your real members are. Let's look at another scripture.

For where your treasure is, there will your heart be also. (Matt. 6:21)

Please understand everyone in your church will not be able to give on the same level. However, everyone should be committed to giving on whatever level they are on. I found, through experience, people who give the most are the most committed. People who give the least are the ones always complaining and hardly ever coming to church. Please understand I do not say this to be disrespectful, but I have found it to be so true. The real givers are in tune with God's program and are willing to do whatever it takes to get better on purpose.

I recall one church my wife and I attended while on vacation. When it was offering time, before the minister could say "It is time for offering," the people began to wave their offering envelopes with great excitement. They were screaming and shouting at the top of their lungs. It sounded like thunder. I saw people get in the aisle, rejoicing in the Spirit. I thought someone had just been filled with the Spirit or had gotten healed and I missed it. Well, to our surprise, it was simply offering time. It was apparent that these members knew the importance of the principles. It was heartfelt, and I almost cried, thinking of how most people feel in my circle when it is offering time. What a refreshing sight; I am purposing in my heart to take some of my key leaders to see these "church offerings" people.

With all this in mind, I can't stress the importance of teaching and training your members on the principles of giving. If you are going to build a church from the ground up, this is very important. Calculate your overhead and know what your budget is. Challenge your people by faith to meet the budget; trust me, someone will step up and say, "I will meet the budget because I want to be blessed by God."

As pastor, you and your church should pray for financial increase. Again, if the tobacco industry and the alcohol industry can reap enormous profits in the middle of a so-called recession, then how much more should God's church be supplied with all it needs to survive? It is truly our kingdom expectation to be able to manage God's church in excellence. God's church should not be just barely surviving; it should be thriving.

Preaching

I understand this is a sensitive area of discussion for most. I certainly will not try to tell you how to preach, neither will I attempt to suggest a certain style of preaching. Every preacher should begin to know and understand his or her limitations as it relates to ministry. However, I do want to caution you on some things that I believe are extremely important for preachers.

Unless you are just extremely prolific in presentation, you will not be able to be effective with long messages in this generation. This is a generation of quick discovery, and no one wants to be preached to for extremely long periods of time. Now, again, unless you really are prolific in your presentation, it will be difficult to get away with long-drawn-out sermons, not to mention you need to leave the room for the altar call.

I would caution you to attempt to preach thirty to forty minutes at most. Then leave the room for the altar so that your total sermon and altar call ranges from forty to fifty minutes. Please understand if you truly can preach and be effective for longer periods of time, please do so. However, consider what I am about to say. Most preachers in smaller churches attempting to build a church from the ground up cannot get away with this. Most times, your members are extremely nice and will not tell you, you preach too long. This is why they do not invite visitors because they will be completely embarrassed at the amount of time spent on preaching.

Another important element of preaching is getting caught up in our preaching styles and abilities that we kick God completely out. In other words, we get in the flesh. We approach the pulpit with the mind-set of "I have it, I am going to rock the house today," when we should approach the sacred desk in reverent fear of God. We should always be praying that the Holy Spirit is able to take over and have his way.

Remember, the service is not about your preaching; it's about the Kingdom of God. If the kingdom is not impacted, then we have not done much of anything. The day and time is out for preaching little cute sermons; people need to be ministered to. This brings me to my next most critical point.

Preaching must be relevant. I recall canvassing the neighborhood, gathering souls for a service. There was lady in particular who I invited to the church we were visiting. She felt in her heart it was time for a change and was compelled to come to the service with us. Once we got her in the service, she really enjoyed herself. When the preacher got up to speak, he spent a good forty-five minutes talking about David killing the giant Goliath. Personally, I believe he wanted to impress the preachers on the pulpit and forgot about the souls God wanted him to minister to. In his efforts to impress us and show us how anointed he was, the opportunity was missed to properly minister to the soul we invited.

Bear in mind he never made the story relevant to us today. Although the visitor enjoyed the service, she told me something else, and I quote, "The preaching was terrible. I did not need to know about David fighting Goliath, I needed to know about my life now." In other words, she realized that she was not going to have to go in the valley and fight anyone. This taught me a very valuable lesson. Preaching must be relevant. Now, the message was cute and well framed, but it was not really relevant to life today. After all, David was in the army, we are not. Maybe if the preacher had drawn some correlations to everyday life, the sermon would have been far more beneficial.

Now, the minister really preached and got anointed. He truly did not even want to stop. However, his preaching only served him and no one else. As God's ministers, we must remember it is not about us.

Years ago, God taught me the importance of changing my message. Let me give you an example. I really like reading and discussing the end-time prophecies. I mean, this is a passion of mine. So every time I preached, most of my messages were end-time in nature. Once, I planned an end-time conference and I thought everyone would be excited about learning about the end-times. I studied and studied and was truly prepared to teach. I studied so hard that I was getting anointed while studying for the teaching. I was so excited about teaching this lesson. Well, on the first night, only one person was in Bible class. Wow, was I disappointed.

I went home that night and prayed. God began to minister to me and said, "The people you are ministering to are not interested in the end-times." They need to know how to get God to pay their gas bill because their gas is off. They need to know how to get God to lead and direct their lives. They need to know how to know they are pleasing God. They needed simple practical teaching designed to educate them on the principles of scripture. This may sound simple, but it is a great revelation.

We must make the Bible applicable to the lives of those we minister to. If not, they will leave guessing. Again, ministry is not about us; it is about the Kingdom of God and the people we minister to. Before we close this portion, I would like to look at one last element.

Make sure you are preaching and teaching the Word. Most of us talk about the Word, but we do not teach the Word. Let me give you an example. You should not get up and say "God wants us to be good stewards." Now, we know this is a true statement, but I can't leave it there. I must also tell them how to be a good steward.

Let me give you another example. We might say "Put on the whole armor of God that you may be able to stand." OK, to me, this sounds like the church has some armor from God in a closet somewhere that I must put on. No, we must tell them about the armor, where to find it, and how to put it on. We cannot assume they know about God's armor. So the Lord taught me to be mindful of statements that I make in the pulpit and never assume people know. They must be taught. Can you see where I'm going with this? We tell people to do a lot of things but never teach them what the Bible says about how to do it. We tell people to live holy, but we fail to tell them how to live holy.

I want to give you another scripture. The Apostle Paul is talking with Timothy. Listen to what he tells him:

> Study to shew thyself approved unto God, a workman that needeth not be ashamed, rightly dividing the word of truth. (2 Tim. 2:15)

Study habits are so important in life. This can be said of anything. Take for example someone studying to become a medical doctor. Well, if they do not study, they will not be a good doctor. They will not be able to pass their test or get through the certifications involved in the profession. What about becoming an attorney? You must study extremely hard because if you don't, you will not make a good attorney. I have had the chance to go to court and witness good attorneys and not-so-good attorneys. Clearly, I have seen how frustrating a bad attorney can be.

Well, what about the ministry of God's Word? Can you see how important it is for us to study and stay in the Word? We have to give ourselves over to prayer and the study of God's Word. Let me give you one more scripture on this note. In Acts, the apostles had a problem with the administration of food, so they appointed deacons to administer the food. Listen to this scripture:

> But we will give ourselves continually to prayer, and to the Ministry of the Word. (Acts 6:4)

Can you see how important this was to the apostles of old? They did not want to engage in anything that took them away from the Word of God. We must allow ourselves time on a daily basis to engage in the Word of God. Sometimes we need to stop preaching so much and get in the Word of God.

Altar Call

Here is another important area of the church experience that I believe is the most important area. The altar call is the time in the service where the Holy Spirit moves upon the hearts of those who are not saved. How we make that invitation is critical to our success in ministry.

Normally, when the altar call is made, there is an automatic assumption that the unsaved understands and knows what it means to accept Christ. Let me give you an example. In one church, the altar call was made, and a lady came down front to accept Christ. Once she got down in front, six altar workers surrounded her; two of them had towels, one of them had a bottle of oil. The rest of them were praying in the Spirit with mean looks on their faces. Trust me, this was not a good sight to see. The other unsaved people who wanted to come down front decided not to come because of the intimidation seeing this caused. Everyone in your congregation may not truly understand what is going to take place during the altar call.

What I've learned to do is explain what is going to happen. So I will say something like this: "There may be someone here that desires to receive the Lord. In a moment I'm going to ask you to come down the aisle, but before I do let me explain what is going to happen."

Then I explain what will happen when they come down the aisle. "When you come down, someone is going to talk to you about given your life to Christ. If it is appropriate, we will pray for you. If not, we will take you in the back and minister more clearly to your needs. If you are here, come right down, the next move is yours."

I have experienced great success when I explain thoroughly what is about to happen. People feel more comfortable when they know you are not going to embarrass or harass them. Now most times, the Holy Ghost will meet the repentant soul. When the Holy Ghost meets someone at the altar, you never have to worry about them because they are enjoying the Holy Spirit tremendously. They will leave extremely happy that they came and gave their lives to Christ.

I believe the altar call has four parts. The first part is to announce to the church that no one should be walking or talking; this is the altar call. This is extremely important because it calls everyone to attention.

The second part of the altar call is to announce the type of altar call you are having. Is it for the saints, the lost, or everyone? Whoever the altar call is for should be announced.

Then you should tell them what the altar call is all about, that you're going to ask them to come down the aisle and what you're going to do when they come down the aisle. This is the time to explain to them that you are not going to embarrass them.

The last thing is to make the call. Once the call is made, give time for the Holy Ghost to work on the hearts of people. An effective altar call can be made in a very brief period of time. It should not be long and drawn out unless God is leading you to prolong.

One thing that I would like to caution smaller growing churches not to do is to overwhelm unbelievers with the pressure of intentionally targeting them in a small setting. If you only have fifty members in your church, it becomes very easy to see who is new and who is not. So by all means, you should keep the altar call as standard as possible. If you overwhelm new visitors, you will lose them, and they will never come back. Unless of course, if God touches their hearts.

Another area of caution in smaller growing churches is to not make an altar call because you have no visitors. Even in times when you do not have a visitor, I would encourage you to still make an altar call, only you make it to the saints. This is important because the altar is the place where lives are changed. Now let's talk about one final area, which is the dismissal.

Dismissal

Another important part of the service is the dismissal. I can't tell you how important the dismissal time has been to me. It gives you a chance to connect with members as well as meet your visitors up close and personal. You can look your members or visitors in the eyes and tell them positive things that will cause a faith reaction. A faith reaction is when someone responds to a God-given statement that you have made.

For example, I like to tell our visitors, "I'm so glad you came." This one statement will go a long way. Or you may say something like "We were so happy to have you in our services." It's something about statements like these that can send a visitor from your service feeling good about coming. Even if they were upset or agitated about something, God has a way of anointing the pastor's words so that they will have impact in the hearts of people. This reminds me of a very powerful scripture in the book of 1 Samuel:

> And Samuel grew and the Lord was with him, and did not let
> none of his words fall to the ground. (1 Sam. 3:19)

God has a way of using our words in special ways. Any opportunity we have to get in front of new visitors is a golden opportunity. Let's be sure to take advantage of every ministry moment that we may have. I am a firm believer that we can minister in and out of the pulpit.

Follow Up a Key Element

Follow-up is an extremely important part of growing your church. It deals with what happens to the visitors once they leave the service. As discussed earlier, you still want to quantify what visitors your church decides to follow up with. For example, I probably will not follow up with a visitor who has a church home and is not interested in changing their membership. Now you can quickly assess this information by talking with the person who invited this guest. Most often, you will find out that they only came because they were friends with someone in your congregation. With that in mind, you may not want to follow up with that individual.

Certainly we can never predict what the Holy Ghost will do, but I am a firm believer that we should not be targeting members from other churches. This practice is never wholesome, especially those who are of the same faith or denomination. Bear in mind, if they just showed up uninvited because they heard or knew about the church, then they should be treated as a regular visitor.

When someone attends your church, it's a priority that you gather some information about that visitor. The goal of gathering information is to be able to send them a follow-up letter thanking them for attending, also to invite them to future services that you may have. It also gives you the opportunity to reach out to these individuals, providing them with information concerning your church. Without their contact information, it will be very difficult to have a direct touch with that visitor again.

Follow-up Process

Each church should have a follow-up process to deal with visitors. Now let me explain that there is no perfect process. I believe we all try out different processes as we go along. I do find that most often, new churches do not have a follow-up process. Some of them have a follow-up committee, which consists of one person who is not really trained to follow up. Neither is there anyone consistently monitoring whether or not the follow-up is effective. With this in mind, it becomes extremely important for the church to have a process that ensures each visitor is receiving the attention that they deserve.

I want to talk about what has been effective for us. Our ushers have been trained to identify visitors and to give them the best seats in the house. Have you ever attended a crowded event? When you arrive at the door, you want someone to greet you. After greeting you, you want them to say "I have reserved a seat just for you." This will not only make them feel important, but it gives a nice tone to a first-time visitor. Ushers should be able to identify people that are first-time comers. I cannot stress how vitally important this is.

Then the usher should ask, "Do you need anything right now?" Most visitors want to know if the person who invited them is present. They might want to know where the washrooms are or if there is a nursery. Whatever the concern is, it should be addressed promptly. Then our visitors are ready to receive because all of their questions and concerns have been addressed right up front. Once rapport is established between our visitors and the ushers, it is now time to invite them to fill out the visitor card.

Here is what has worked fairly well in our midst. As a church, we like to send letters, a CD, or video e-mails as a special gift to first-time visitors. The idea here is you send them something just to appreciate their coming. This is a wonderful idea for any church that is growing and on the move for God. Every time you have an opportunity to touch your visitor is a ministry moment. Even if they do not come right back to your church, you position your church in their hearts. So the next time they are having a difficult time, hopefully they will think of your church.

As pastor, you can mail them a "from the desk of" note, writing in your own handwriting. This is powerful because now your visitor knows you are truly thinking of them.

By now, you should get my point. Once that visitor comes in through the door, it is time to start building the relationship that is so vital to church growth.

I learned in a seminar at Moody Bible Institute that most people are more comfortable joining a church where they know someone. This is another reason why your members should invite people to church. When your members invite people to church, the potential of them staying is extremely high because they know someone in the congregation. Now you have an advantage of working with this new visitor. They already know someone within your church who is comfortable. Now all you have to do is your part in making them feel welcome, and God will do the rest.

You will be amazed at how the Holy Ghost will begin to compel people to salvation. Please understand, the Holy Ghost can draw them whether we do our part or not. However, I believe we work along with God when we do our part. In John 6:44, there is a very moving passage of scripture that I believe speaks to the treatment of our visitors.

> No man can come to Me, except the father which has sent Me
> draw him: and I will raise him up at the last day.

Based upon this scripture, we have to understand that if God drew them, they are God's guests. If visitors are God's guests, then we must treat them with the utmost respect. The latter part of this verse says, "I will raise them up at the last day." Wow, this is critical. It's a matter of eternal life. Listen, we must do our part.

The Visitor Form

The form that the visitor fills out is equally as important. We have customized our visitor's card to meet the needs of our church. I also encourage you to do the same. Look at the example below.

Faith Cathedral Visitor's Card	Input By	Called By
	Notes:	Yearly #

On behalf of Faith Cathedral Church, we would like to thank you for visiting with us

Mr
Mrs
Miss First and Last Name _____ Date _____
Address _____
City _____ State _____ Zip Code _____
Apartment or Complex # _____
I am a guest of _____
I am a member of what church _____ None _____
    (If not a member of any church, circle—None—)
Do you have school-age children? Yes _____ No _____
Do you have an e-mail address? _____
Telephone _____

Help us understand your needs (check one below)

_____	Would like more information about the church?
_____	Would like information about becoming a member?
_____	Would like to meet with the pastor or minister?
_____	Would like to know how to improve my life?
_____	Would like to be placed on the e-mail mailing list?
_____	Would like a call from the pastor or a minister of the church?

This card allows us to quickly gather information. The name is important because the ushers should be trained to remember their names immediately. When the service is over, it is a powerful thing to be able to call a visitor by name and tell them, "We certainly enjoyed you being with us."

The address gives you a flavor for what it takes for this person to get to your church. Location is extremely important. I remember we once had a visitor who attended our service. After service, I discovered that she lived in another state. According to her testimony, she really enjoyed the services and wanted to come again. In fact, she said to me, "I will drive up every Sunday." Now, she was clearly over one hundred miles away. I knew this would not work. I knew of another pastor near her place of residence, and I referred her to his church. In this instance, we have no need to send a special gift or CD. Her location would be too costly for her to come every week. She will be better served with a church closer to her home. This is why I like to know where a person lives.

On the form that we use, it asks them very plainly if they have a church home. This is very important to know because it tells you a lot more about the visitor. If they do not have a church home, just maybe God has called them to your church for such a time as this. It could be that they have never been in church before. Whatever the case, this person is a great candidate for God to save and use in the Kingdom of God. Considering the fact that she is at your church, it makes all the sense to me that God can use them there.

Now this question flows very well with the altar call. When I do the altar call, there is a statement I normally make. "It is the will of God that you spend your Christian experience in a local church." I go on to say, "If you don't have a church home, you need one." You will be amazed at how people are looking for someone just to invite them to join. I certainly understand that it's more to church than just saying "I'm willing to join." However, when a person is willing, then I can discuss everything else with them. Things like being saved and what it means to repent. This simply opens the door for conversation.

When you are starting a church from the ground up, you must be willing to work with people. I have learned not to be so locked in when working with people. We have in our midst right now a precious young lady who joined our church in body form first. She has been attending for about six months now. Just recently, God filled her with the Holy Spirit. Most times, people do not do well when a lot of rules are tossed at them right away. Long story short, she is happy, saved, and redeemed. What joy we get when lives are truly being changed.

Now, I would like to address the questions on the visitor cards. There are six additional questions we ask our visitors to respond to. For purposes of this book, I would like to address each one individually and how you can use the information gathered.

The first question is, "Would you like more information about the church?" This is a very valuable question. People come with all kinds of experiences, and if they are considering attending your church, sometimes they have questions. We have put together a short and simple brochure that tells a bit about the pastor and some of the ministries we have in our church. This information is mailed out to the visitors. However, before it gets mailed, we have a person who places a phone call to this visitor just as a follow-up on what they checked off in the service.

We have customized a special script for the call that should be followed at all times. Again, this is important because whoever is designated to place this call must know what they are doing. In the appendix section of this book, I have an example of a phone script to address this specific question.

In providing visitors with information, we stay away from all doctrinal issues that lead to debates and, in many instances, will be a turnoff to the visitor. For example, if your information has things like "You must be born-again," or "What in hell do you want," or "All liars shall have their part in the lake that burns with fire and brimstone." Because people are not quick to adapt to truth, these statements might drive them away. I can't help but remember the scripture that says, "He who wins souls is wise."

Now, we understand that these may be true statements, but they do nothing to edify a new comer. We should focus on information that edifies. When a Burger Joint advertises their burgers, they don't discuss anything about fat grams. You never hear them say, "This burger has fourteen fat grams, and you will gain weight." Maybe this is not the best example, but you get the point. Any information you send out should serve to edify.

The next question we ask is "Would you like information on becoming a member?" Not every first-time visitor is going to get up and come down the aisle on Sunday morning. If this is their first visit, they may not be ready to get up in front of everyone and come down the aisle.

If they check off the statement concerning information on being a member, it is a great indication to me that this person is interested in joining our church. It also lets me know that they truly enjoyed the visit with us.

Again, we have a very simple brochure that also tells the benefits of becoming a member. Keep in mind there should be a benefit that results in being a member of your church.

It makes no difference how big or small your church is; if people are willing to become members, they must have an ample understanding of what this means. I like to explain that becoming a member works in two stages. We have what I would like to call formal membership. Formal membership is when someone unsaved decides "This will be my church home." They may not have even been baptized yet. They just start coming to church and liking what God is starting to do in their lives. Then there is what I call spiritual membership. Spiritual Membership is when a person submits himself or herself to God's salvation plan. These are people who have repented and are baptized in water and the Holy Ghost. Then this person becomes a member of the body of Christ, because now their spirit has been redeemed. This kind of membership no one can take from an individual.

You will be amazed at the many people who do not understand membership and the benefits associated with the kind of membership that they desire. I often ask visitors what kind of membership they are looking for. This is important because some people are very emotional, and they make emotional commitments that do not last. So you must clearly understand what your visitors are looking for in a church. This way, you will avoid the trap of people professing to have joined the church but not being faithful to their commitment.

Once again, we follow up with this visitor by way of a phone call. I've provided a script in the index portion of this book for your consideration. At least it gives you a process to follow and a procedure to uphold. We have had great results using these methods so far. This is the reason why I felt it so necessary to put this information in a book. I believe another thriving church can benefit from it as well. Now let's move to the next statement.

The next statement is, "I would like to meet with the pastor or minister of the church." If someone checks off this statement, it's a great indication to me that they really need something. I or one of our ministers can use this opportunity to personally witness to this individual. They may have a simple need that they want met. If the need is within reason, then we can do it. Now I discourage any new or thriving church to start handing out money. No visitor meets with me after a visit or two and I become willing to give them money! This is a huge no-no. If you do that, you will have several more of these meetings where people are only looking for money.

When I talk about people having a need to be met, I'm talking about needing good sound advice, or maybe they have something personal to tell you that they do not feel comfortable talking to anyone else. The key emphasis is creating the right atmosphere and inviting people to be comfortable sharing the problems of their lives. These meetings can be very powerful.

I recall such a meeting with one of our current parishioners when they first came to the church. They were sick and needed God to help them. It just so happened that the church they use to attend does not allow them to talk directly to their pastor. Therefore, they were invited to come and talk to me through one of our members. Again, it was a divine moment as God ministered and touched them. It was because of such a meeting they are still with us today. This was truly one of those divine moments wherein God worked to add to our church.

I encourage you, if your church is growing, be touchable. The time to be important and untouchable will truly come. When God elevates your ministry where you have so many people it becomes impossible for you to meet with them all, then he will provide you with capable ministers to help you.

The next statement I would like to address is, "I would like to know how to improve my life." Now this statement is designed to locate people who are searching. They may not be 100 percent ready to give their lives to the Lord, but they are searching. I've prepared a very special video presentation that I can send to them directly through their e-mail.

During this presentation, I try to minister very briefly to our visitors in a very personal and direct way. Without going into the details of the video, let me highlight the format.

I start the presentation off by telling them how glad I am that they had an opportunity to attend one of our services. Then I highlight the fact that this is a very short video to set their hearts at ease. Then I try to do three things. One, I want to encourage them by speaking a word of faith into their lives. Two, I want to instruct them in very simple steps on how to change their lives. Lastly, I want to invite them with a salvation invitation filled with the benefits from the Word of God.

You just got to hear it. The unique thing about this e-mail is that you can see whether or not they have watched the video. From time to time, if they have not watched the video, I can resend it with a special note requesting them to watch it.

Once I know a visitor has seen the video, then the follow-up team places a call to them, thanking them for taking the time to watch the video. It is during this call that we also reach out and invite them back to the church. Remember, the more you touch people, the more comfortable they become with you. This is just another way of reaching people. As a growing church, we must work with God to reach out beyond the walls of our local assembly.

Our fifth statement is, "I would like to be placed on the e-mail list." This is a list where we notify visitors when we are having services or communicate events or community services that our visitors need to be aware of.

Many times, people will respond to your e-mail with a prayer request and other things, allowing you to have another touch with that visitor. With the visitor's e-mail address, you are sure to be able to keep contact with them at all times. This is very practical and important to understand. E-mails are virtually free advertising and will work to advertise your event. Your goal should be to really build your e-mail list up so that on a monthly basis, you can connect with those visitors that just have not returned back to your services.

The next statement on the visitor's card is "I would like a call from the pastor or minister of the church." Again, this is a door opener for the church to truly get to know the visitor. I'm always excited when visitors request a call. I understand that this is the perfect opportunity to win a soul.

Can you see how much detail we put into the outreach area of our church? It is our responsibility to follow up. God is not coming down from heaven to follow up with visitors, neither is God going to make one phone call to anyone. If follow-up is going to get done, it will take the passion of the pastor and their staff to do it.

Presence of the Spirit

One of the most important aspects of church growth is the presence of the Spirit. Remember, the church in the book of Acts had a heavy presence of the Spirit of God. I would like to give you a scripture of support for what I am about to say:

> And they went forth, and preached every where, the Lord working with them, and confirming the word with signs following. (Mark 16:20)

The scripture says that God was working with them. That's so important to remember. The scripture says God worked with them, not God did it for them. God worked with them as they worked, confirming his word with signs following.

The ministry of the Holy Ghost is so important in the church. In most of our services, the operation of the Holy Spirit is overlooked. I encourage every pastor to pray before every service, requesting the Holy Ghost to have his way.

Acts records the activating of the Holy Ghost working with the church. Jesus told his disciples to wait for the promise of the Father.

> And, being assembled together with them, commanded them that they should not depart from Jerusalem, but wait for the promise of the Father, which, saith he, ye have heard of me. (Acts 1:4)

Jesus understood how vitally important it was to have the power of the Spirit working in your life. Jesus told the disciples that they would get the power to witness. Spirit-inspiring witnessing cannot be omitted in the growing of a Spirit-filled church. It was in the plan of God to have people filled with the Holy Ghost who would not only tell the story, but will have the power behind the story.

I remember when I first heard a young man testify who had recently been filled with the Holy Ghost. It was one of the most powerful things I had ever heard. His words moved me to conviction. Immediately, I found myself saying, "This is what I desire when I get saved." I wanted the power of God in my life.

Peter, on the day of Pentecost, had the power of God in his life. In fact, in Acts chapter 2, he was given a message inspired by the Holy Ghost that caused about three thousand souls to be added to the church. Do you realize that one Holy Ghost—inspired message can cause souls to be added to the church? This makes fellowship with the Holy Ghost so important for every witness, every preacher, and believer. After we witness and people come to church, only God can cause souls to be added to the church. Look at the scripture:

> But now hath God set the members every one of them in the body, as it hath pleased him. (1 Cor. 12:18)

It is almost as if God is placing people where he wants them to be, like a well-put-together puzzle. So when new people come into your church, do not allow this to be a prideful moment. This is an opportunity for God to bless your church in ways that you would have never imagined.

Avoiding the Trap of Pride

I would like to point out one thing. For pastors, pride is an issue. Every pastor must deal with the pride in their hearts. God is not interested in growing your church if you are full of pride. This is a satanic trap that must be avoided. The way you avoid the trap of pride is to continue to work for the Lord. Serve God with all of your heart, and never talk about what the

Lord is doing for your church. Let others talk about it, but you should never go around saying, "Look at what God is doing in my church."

Some pastors I talk to start out right away, telling me what meetings they have to go to at their church. Or they discuss with me what they preached about and who got saved. Now, we know that there is nothing really wrong with that. However, it will be better served coming from others. I would like to show you a scripture concerning this:

> Let another man praise thee, and not thine own mouth; a stranger, and not thine own lips. (Prov. 27:2)

Look at what this scripture says: "Let another man praise thee, and not thine own mouth." Typically, when you praise yourself, it denotes pride. It is best to just go on and allow God to bless your church.

I recall one pastor who had told me all of the wonderful things that God was doing at his church. When that day came that I would have an opportunity to visit his church, he made every excuse as to why I should not come. I truly believe he did not want me to see that the things he told me about were not all that he said it was.

Some pastors brag about how many members they have. Again, this is gross immaturity and a great indication that pride has taken hold of them. I can't stress this principle enough. Stay away from pride at all costs. If you feel pride trying to creep into your heart, then get a mop and a pail or just take a toothbrush and start scrubbing the floor and praying, all at the same time. You must humble yourself under the mighty hand of God. Now, maybe it does not take all of the scrubbing for you, but certainly you get my point. God hates pride.

Avoid the Sabotage of Sexual Impurity

Certainly this is one of the least discussed subjects among clergy, but yet it is one of the most dangerous sabotages of church growth. Every inspiring young pastor has to learn to manage lust. Understand it is Satan's desire to sabotage the spirit of your church. Sexual impurity is sternly addressed in scripture, and we are warned to stay away. I want to give you a scripture that I believe is key.

> But every man is tempted, when he is drawn away of his own lust, and enticed. Then when lust has conceived, it brings forth sin: and sin, when it is finished, brings forth death. (James 1:14-15)

Listen to this scripture, emphasis on "every man is tempted." This plainly tells us that every man is tempted. As leaders, we must learn to manage our lust so that it does not get out of control. Now understand, lust works in all kind of ways. It works with eating, the flesh, and greed. It must be managed. For purpose of this paragraph, let's look at it from a sexual perspective.

In the area of sex, it is critical that you invest into your marriage. Never neglect the importance of partnering with your spouse to help discuss and manage your lust. Now, I realize this might be a bit too real for most people, but these are the things that pastors, especially new pastors, need instructions on. Early on, God gave me a lust plan. A lust plan is an action plan designed to help you manage your lust.

Now, before I talk about the lust plan that I use, consider this. The devil is going to fight the leader in the area of lust. The fight is intense and sometimes can be clearly overwhelming. Now let me ask you a question: do you have lust? Just consider what I am about to say. More than likely, your answer is yes. It might be under control, but you have it. Every now and then, Satan is going to see if it is still buried. He will constantly try to conceive it or birth it in you. Here is how the scripture says it "when lust has conceived." When it is birthed, it brings forth sin. The scripture goes on to say, "Do not err, my beloved brethren."

You don't have to look far in the body of Christ to see how the devil has attacked many of our fellow clergy. Some of the brethren are public figures, exposed on television and radio. Others are not as public, but the family and church effects are still extremely hurting. Acts of adultery, pornography, gay and lesbianism have chipped away at the conviction of leaders. With that in mind, it becomes extremely important that you have a lust plan. After all, what would happen if you find yourself being tempted or your lust is out of control? I mean, think about it; what would you do? Most would say just pray about it. Or you need to fast to beat the flesh under control. Certainly we know these are the spiritual weapons that we should use. However, there are some other things in addition to fasting and prayer that I would certainly recommend.

Years ago, I was in a marriage seminar taught by an older precious mother who has since passed on. In the seminar, there was a couple who had been married for about three years. The husband shared a personal testimony that changed my life. He shared that there was a woman on his job who was very attractive. She was doing everything she could to get to him. After weeks of being tempted, he was feeling like he was going to be overthrown. He and his wife had been having the normal struggles of marriage. Getting to work and seeing this other lady seemed to be a breath of fresh air to him. After all, she was nice, pretty, and very soft-spoken, according to him.

He further explained that he got to the point where he wanted to talk with her more. Even while being at home, his mind was constantly on this other lady. One day, after leaving an anointed service, he was convicted and cried out to God about the matter. He explained that he loved his wife but was simply struggling with lust.

According to him, after crying out about the matter, he said God told him to tell his wife about it. Now, to most, this is very difficult because the wife is going to feel as if it is a slap in her face. After all, he should not be looking at another woman. On top of that, he is supposed to be saved. In his heart, he felt he wanted to be free, so he needed to share it with his wife before anything happened. He explained he would rather tell her prior to something happening than to wait until something happens.

So that is what he did. He told his wife that he was being tempted beyond what he felt he could bear. At first, his wife was upset and extremely angry. However, because God had told him to share it, before the day was out, the wife had gotten over the anger and respected the fact that he had come to her. While in the seminar, she spoke out about it as well. She said that she was angry, but then she began to understand. She explained that he did the right thing. Most men wait until they have committed some sinful act to expose the secrets of the heart, but her husband was up front.

So they got together and began to pray. Her husband said immediately, the bands of that lust that had gripped him was broken, and he felt himself being free. Even when he returned to work to face the same lady, his heart had been completely delivered. He no longer faced that lust, and he and his wife had received a wonderful testimony of deliverance.

After hearing such a wonderful story, I was compelled to adopt the same philosophy in my marriage. Now please understand, you don't run to your spouse and tell them every time you have a bad thought. That's not what I'm trying to say. I'm talking about prolonged developed lust that has gripped your heart and is about to overthrow you if God does not deliver. Let's face it, if anybody knows when you are about to do wrong, it is you.

Sexual impurity is a cancer in the body of Christ among leadership, and it must be dealt with. This is why I stress the emphasis of having a lust plan. You need to know what to do if you find yourself in such a situation. To some, this might be a bit too real, but it is true. We have an enemy, and one of his primary attacks is to pollute the church with sexual impurity. Let's look at another scripture found in 2 Corinthians 2:11:

> Lest Satan should get an advantage of us: for we are not ignorant of his devices.

I place special emphasis on the word *devices*. Satan has devices that he will use in the church to deceive, pollute, and rob the church of its integrity. If a church loses its integrity, it will have a very difficult time recovering from it. It is certainly not impossible because in the body of Christ, other leaders have recovered themselves from it. However, it is a road of pain that you certainly want to avoid. Now, let's talk about a lust plan.

Lust Plan

The first thing you must do is make a decision to live holy. Once you have truly made this decision, then it is very difficult to be tempted. How can you be tempted when you have already made a decision? Of course, Satan is going to shoot at you with thoughts, but when you have made a decision, you can quickly dismiss them and move on. The emphasis here is to make the decision.

The second thing you want to do is covenant with your spouse that you can always come to them before anything happens. Notice I said before, not after. You should have healthy relations with your spouse, and your spouse should have the maturity to understand certain things. If you have a spouse in leadership, the enemy will try to use his devices. Let me give you an example of how the conversation should go.

You go to your spouse and say, "Hey, I'm really in a battle, and I need you to pray with me. I've been wrestling in the area of my lust, and I need you to partner with me to fight this thing."

You don't have to go into too much detail, such as who it is or what is actually tempting you. That's not important. The important part is that you have a partner or a helpmeet to fight sexual impurity in your church. I truly believe once you have enlisted the support of your spouse, God is going to break that thing right away. "What the Lord has joined together, let no man put asunder."

The third thing you must do is work with a spiritual other, typically your pastor or your mother or an aged spiritual person that God has placed in your life to help you. The good thing about God is he has already placed people within your life to help you. You just have to look around; God has already placed someone in your life that you can discuss your battles with. Do not try to be a superman or super holy, because your flesh is not saved.

Some pastors make the terrible mistake of not praying and fasting. It is amazing, but it is true. After preaching so long and especially if God has favored you with a few members, it is easy to neglect the basics. The basics of prayer and fasting is essential to your leadership. Personally, my wife and I still go to prayer every Tuesday.

I had the unique privilege to grow up under great men of God, men who stayed in prayer. Every time I think about this, it fills my heart with joy. These praying men taught me so much about staying in prayer. They lived holy lives before me from week to week, month to month, and year to year. I could depend on what they told me, because I watched them live it before my eyes. I thank God to this day for the deposit that these great men of

God left in my life. Truly, they have helped shape me into the man of God that I am today.

Now there are others who do not share my experience and did not grow up in a prayerful, holy environment. What are they to do? This is why I've spent so much time talking about the importance of having a plan before time to deal with your lust. Let me give you another scripture, penned by one of the greatest apostles ever, the Apostle Paul.

> For I know that in me [that is, in my flesh], dwells no good thing: for to will is present with me; but how to perform that which is good I find not. For the good that I would I do not: but the evil which I would not, that I do. Now if I do that I would not it is no more I that do it, but sin that dwells in me. (Rom. 7:18-20)

Here is the Apostle Paul expressly saying he had to struggle with his sin nature. This is the man that Jesus knocked off his beast in the ninth chapter of Acts. This is the man that had heavenly vision up into the third heaven. This is the man that was completely sold out to God. Yet we find him talking about the struggle with the sin nature. Please understand if it was a struggle for Paul, surely we will not escape. Even still, we know we can overcome because of a great cloud of witnesses who have already overcome. It is certainly my prayer that this information ministers to your heart and gives you the information you need to make it.

God Is in the Soul-saving Business

You got to remember God is in the soul-saving business. Look at what the scriptures says in John 3:16:

> For God so loved the world, that he gave his only begotten Son, that whosoever believeth in him should not perish, but have everlasting life.

God wants people to believe in him. This is what church growth is all about. Growing a church is not about becoming a big preacher or having an opportunity to brag on how much God has done. Neither is it a chance for us to showcase our talents and abilities. Neither should we be in discussion about how many members we have or how large our church facility is. This is a chance for us to display the love of God in the earth through the power of the Holy Ghost. Just as God is concerned about souls, we must also be concerned about souls.

Every morning, I make it a practice to pray. Not just praying to say I prayed or to feel spiritual; however, my prayers are designed to ask God for direction. I need to know from God every day what his desire is for me. We are God's tools of salvation in the earth, and we must stay continually in his face for direction. Now, I want to talk about some other ways to get people in your church that are very inexpensive but yet very effective.

Church Growth Elements

If you are starting to read this section, then I'm confident that you are interested in growing your church. I want to take a moment to encourage every parishioner and every pastor to let you know it is not hopeless. Regardless of your current situation, things can turn around for you. I want to ask you to consider the following church growth strategies. I believe they can work for anyone that will prayerfully work them.

One of the main questions for pastors is, "How do I get people in the doors from week to week?" Earlier in the book, we talked about the law of numbers and how effective it is to just invite people. Again, this is the most cost-effective way to witness or, what I like to call it, market your church. Word of mouth by far is the most powerful form of advertising there is. As mentioned earlier, the first strategy is to just invite people. How many people can your congregation commit to inviting each week?

Family and Friends Day

Family and friends day is always a unique way to get people you know familiarize with your church. Most of us have family and friends that we are in good standings with. These are people who would not mind attending an event that has been specifically designed for them. Now, I am a person that believes in getting results. With that in mind, I am not interested in inviting family members who are already committed to a church. My target would be family and friends who are not currently committed to a church. This is of great importance, because we need proper soil to plant a seed.

I instruct our members to target the right family and friends who are the unchurched, untaught, and uncommitted. Then I like to have a period of cultivation. Here is what I mean by cultivation. If you do not have a ready relationship with the person of interest in your family, then they are not going to be willing to come to church. Our cultivation period may start anywhere from a year to six months before any invitation is placed in their hands.

Cultivation means calling them on their birthdays and possibly even going out to lunch or dinner with them. You may just call them once a week for small talk. The key emphasis is targeting that soul for salvation. The emphasis here is building a relationship. Talking to that person more than just about church. If you do that and it is genuine, then people will be more willing to come to a church event that you invite them to.

Teach your people to cultivate before asking family or friends to attend a service. This is so important and powerful as a concept. Let me give you an example of this. I used to work in the insurance industry. While working in the insurance industry, we had a night where we would cold-call prospects. The thing that made it a cold call was the fact that we did not know any of these people; we just picked up the phone and called. Well, as you may guess, if you relied on this method for reaching new prospects, you would not be in business very long.

In our training, they taught us to make warm calls. Warm calls were to our family and friends, people who we were familiar with. People who new us and would be willing to help us. Certainly, it was true; warm calls were always likely to turn into something positive. Cold-calling was like taking a chance, almost liking guessing. I believe we can use this same information while working with souls.

Do not just invite your family and friends to church. Start building a relationship with them before inviting them to church. It will make the invitation much more inviting. The people you invite will consider that you already care about them and are not just trying to save them.

I want to make this statement again, just to drive my point. The people you invite will consider that you already care about them and are not just trying to save them. This is so vitally important.

I can certainly recall our first family and friends day. It was just that, a day where our family and friends came out to see the church and support those of us who are loved. It was not an outreach opportunity for saving souls. Since then, I have learned to be more outreach minded in my efforts. This is why I place great emphasis on unchurched, untaught, and unsaved. These are the people who will be great prospects for growing your church. In short, family and friend days can be effective growth elements but must be targeted to invite the unchurched, untaught, and unsaved.

OUTREACH CAMPAIGNS

Another element of church growth is a dynamic outreach campaign. In order to have an effective outreach campaign, you must supply a solution to the needs of your community. With the proper solution, you will draw the right people. In order for you to properly understand what an effective campaign is, I want to start out by giving you an example.

A couple of years ago, we had a diaper drive. During the diaper drive, we supplied diapers to all mothers between the ages of twenty-five and younger, who were single with children. If you were a mother and you needed diapers, you were required to register for the event. We had a huge overflow of young mothers register for this event. So as you can see, we had a proper target.

Knowing who your target is, is vitally important when you are working with campaigns. This is just one example of how to get people into your church. Now the people that came to get the diapers were ministered to, and we had opportunity to get their contact information so that we could network and invite more people to the cause of Christ.

Our current members at the time canvassed the area and passed out flyers regarding the diaper drive. The flyers supplied all the information needed, including a phone number for the mothers to register. We had many mothers call in and register for the diaper drive. The event was a huge success. We ministered to those young mothers, and many of them came back to church or sent their children to our church many days after. Can you see it? It gives your church a face in the community and exposure with more people. Trust me, this is exactly what you need to stimulate growth in the church.

Another campaign that we did was "a large block festival." We closed off the street where our church was located and brought in a dunk tank, basketball hoops, a boxing ring, and many other things that the community could enjoy. Midway through the fun, we stopped everything and preached the Word. We have found that people are very receptive and eager to hear what we have to say. It gives us great exposure, and people begin to see how nice we are as a church. No longer could the neighbors sit in the sidelines, wondering what kind of church is that on the corner. We painted their perception of us for them by reaching out to them.

I will never forget that event. Truly, God smiled upon us, as we had many visitors for weeks after that event. Some of the people on the block even began to pay their tithes to our church. It was amazing how visitors would simply drop their tithes in our mail slot. When the community knows the church in their neighborhood, there is a friendly smell that goes out from the church. The cause of Christ is exalted, and people are willing to get involved.

The goal of the campaigns is to get guests in our services. We certainly accomplished our goal, as we had visitors for weeks following this event.

I believe outreach campaigns, when done properly, are one of the most effective elements of church growth. However, they must be done effectively. You must have the right target and create the proper objective. Without the proper target and objective, you will not be able to fulfill the purpose of your campaign.

Launching the Outreach Campaign

Now I would like to spend some time talking about how to properly launch an outreach campaign. It works best when we start with the Word of God. Let me give you a scripture that I believe would be perfect for the campaign:

> And the lord said unto the servant, Go out into the highways and hedges, and compel them to come in, that my house may be filled. (Luke 14:23)

Using this scripture as a biblical basis to launch your campaign is great because we have Jesus, the author of our faith, encouraging us to go out and compel them to come! I like what the latter part of the scripture says: "that my house may be filled." God wants his house filled. Not just barely making it, but he wants his house to be filled. You may feel like this is impossible, but with God, all things are possible.

So your first course of action is starting with the Word of God. The Word of God is the lamp that lights our faith.

Teaching

The second thing that you must do is start teaching outreach from the Word of God. There are so many scriptures that you can use to teach your membership the responsibility of believers to reach out to the lost. Certainly, we understand that reaching the lost was important to Jesus. In his final command to us before he ascended up, he left these words:

> Go ye therefore, and teach all nations baptizing them in the name of the Father, and of the Son, and of the Holy Ghost; Teaching them to observe all things whatsoever I have commanded you: and, lo, I am with you always, even unto the end of the world. (Matt. 28:19-20)

Since we can clearly see this aspect of Bible instruction is important, we must teach it to our members. Getting the membership ready and comfortable with campaign-focused ministry is key.

Some churches may want to have a focus meeting with their key leaders. You certainly can do that; however, this type of ministry is for everyone. I would be more inclined to get everyone involved as opposed to singling out leaders.

Please understand you must teach on it for more than just a week. I would try to teach on it at least a month, maybe even six weeks. You must thoroughly saturate your congregation with outreach.

Marketing

I like to look at marketing from two focuses. The first focus is internal marketing. Internal marketing is marketing that needs to take place inside the church for the current membership. Here are a couple of key ideas. Hang a banner in the church, something announcing that the campaign is coming. The banner should have a date, a theme, and a scripture. You could also order some pens or something inexpensive, with the name of your church and outreach campaign on it.

Here is my point. The campaign must be different from just another announcement on Sunday morning. You should do something to differentiate this announcement from anything else.

The next focus of marketing is external marketing. External marketing is making sure that your people have the right props for inviting people to the church. For example, they need to know what type of service it is going to be. They need to know what kind of teaching will take place on the night you are expecting your visitors. Your teaching should have an element in it called "what's in it for me." "What's in it for me?" is the question that visitors will be trying to answer when they receive the invitation. If you remember earlier, I told you not to just invite people to church; you must invite them to a cause.

Let me give you some examples of teaching themes that are effective:

> "Come learn what you can do on earth, that will cause God to do something in heaven."

> "Learn principles that will give you victory over poverty."

> "Finding God's plan in tough financial times."

Now, when people get the invitation to your service, the stage is set. They know they are coming to learn from the Word of God. They understand that they will get a benefit from coming. Let's take the last theme for example: "Finding God's plan in tough financial times."

During this series, I am going to discuss the fact that God has a financial plan for his people. I understand that most people do know where to start when it comes to finances in the Bible. So when the invitation is made, the membership has something to say to them other than just inviting them to church. They can simply say, "Come and learn how to find the plan of God in these tough financial times."

During the lesson, the Holy Ghost will work with you and allow things to be said that will always point people to the cross. Our church has been blessed just by working ministry this way. Information is powerful, and when people are informed, then they make better decisions.

The membership needs to be able to know what time the service will start and what time it will end. This is important to first-time visitors. Once the expectation is set, then they come prepared to stay the distance.

So the external marketing is simply having a clearly informed plan as to how the services, meetings, etc., will flow. This way, everyone knows how it will go and can properly communicate to the guests. You should probably even have flyers that your people can pass out.

One thing that you must remember, do not embarrass your members' guests with foolishness. I say this because if the membership loses confidence, they will not invite people for fear of being embarrassed.

Once we get the visitors in the door, we have done our part. The rest is up to God, as he is the only one that can give increase.

Passion

Now there is one element of the outreach campaign that no plan can teach, and that is passion. Without proper passion flowing from the campaign, it will be reduced to a meaningless set of duties designed to fail. You as the pastor and your church members need to be passionate in the things of God.

Find ways to inspire your people to passion. I like to find moving video clips off YouTube and other places that will help our people to understand why we must take action. Remember, outreach involves more than just getting your people involved; it calls for getting them into passion. They must be passionate about that kid whose parents abandoned him at home because of crack cocaine. They must become passionate about the thirteen-year-old boy who was shot to death. Passion stems from a deep desire to do something.

They must become passionate when they see empty seats in the church and no one is present to fill them. They must become passionate about filling up the Sunday school department. They must become passionate about working in youth ministry, instilling in young people a God consciousness.

After reading this information, you should feel pretty good. You should feel good because now you have a plan. You're not just having church; your church has a plan.

Making a Confident Altar Call

Now I have already addressed the elements of the altar call in an earlier section of the book. I just want to encourage you here to make a confident altar call. Feel strong telling people God can change their lives and solve their problems. This confidence is key to the success of any ministry.

FAITH

Faith, by far, is the most important element needed in church growth. You must be able to believe that God can grow your church. Let's look at a very familiar passage of scripture found in Hebrews 11:6:

> But without faith it is impossible to please Him: for he who comes
> to God must believe that He is, and that He is a rewarder of them
> who diligently seek Him.

I want to place great emphasis on the *must believe* portion of this scripture. You must believe that God is able to grow your church and prosper your doings. Now let me examine another passage of scripture that I believe is key as well:

> Now faith is the substance of things hoped for, the evidence of
> things not seen. For by it the Elders obtained a good report. (Heb.
> 11:1-2)

Again, I would like to place emphasis on *substance of things hoped for*. Faith becomes my replacement until the thing that I desire from God gets here. Let me give you an example. While working for Prudential Financial, we received every week what is called a pace report. The pace report was a statement of the commission we were to receive, coupled with any bonuses we had attained. Well, the pace report was not the actual money in the bank, but it served as a replacement until the money hit the account. In fact, I could start saying what bills I was going to pay in advance because I looked at the pace report. I believed the pace report could not lie and what it said I had, I had.

The pace report told me what I could do. I found out through my pace report that I could purchase that five-hundred-dollar television. I found out by my pace report that I could get my wife's hair done, no problem. My pace report told me everything I could have and do. My pace report was the substance of what I was hoping for and the evidence of the money I could not see. Can you see that?

Let me give you another example. I have a MasterCard. My credit limit on this particular card is eleven hundred dollars. I do not have eleven hundred dollars when I walk into a store. I only have the card. So the card is my substance of hope that the eleven hundred dollars is available to me. If I lose my credit card, I lose the confidence that I need because the card is my substance, my evidence of the money not seen.

Well, this is how faith works. Your faith is the substance or the evidence that you have the thing you are hoping for in God. Until the thing actually manifests in the physical, then you must keep your faith. Your faith is the proof that you have it.

You must take your faith as proof that your church is growing, even when you are seeing empty seats every Sunday. This is important because faith without works is dead being alone. We have spent the greater portion of the book giving you the works, but now you need to add your faith to your works.

> What does it profit, my Brethren, though a man say he has Faith, and have not works? Even so faith, if it has not works, is dead, being alone. (James 2:14, 17)

So now we understand we must put the faith and the works together. Now this leads us to a great principle that I would like to highlight.

It is the order of God to always ask us to do something in faith before he does something. Notice in the salvation process, we are instructed to repent first. Everyone has to repent; it is a requirement of salvation before the blessing comes.

God asked Noah to build and ark before the rain came. Remember, it had never rained before, so Noah had to believe what God said, he would bring it to pass.

What about the widow woman at Zarephath? God commanded this woman with no money to sustain the prophet Elijah. When Elijah arrived at Zaraphath, he called and told the widow woman to get him some water. She had no problem with that. As she was going to get the water, he told her to bring him a morsel of bread. Notice the tragic story she tells him.

> And she said, As the Lord your God lives, I have not a cake but an handful of meal in a barrel, and a little oil in a cruse: and, behold, I am gathering two sticks, that I may go in and dress if for me and my son, that we may eat it, and die. (1 Kings 17:12)

She tells Elijah, the man of God, she and her son are on their last leg. She explains that they are down to nothing and getting ready to die. The prophet then tells her to fix his food first. Can you see this? Let's keep looking.

Remember the battle of Jericho, where God told Joshua he had given him the land:

> And the Lord said unto Joshua, See, I have given into your hand Jericho, and the king thereof, and the mighty men of valour. (Josh. 6:2)

I could imagine Joshua shouting and being so excited. However, God says, "Wait one minute", there is something that you must do to get it." God instructs him to get seven priests and the men of war. They were to march around the city once for six days, and on the seventh day, seven times. Then the priests were to blow the horns.

I can easily see Joshua saying, "God, why do you have to send us through all of this? Just let us go in and fight and kill the people." However, the principle is God always requires an act of faith.

Look at the scripture in Matthew 6:33:

But seek you first the Kingdom of God and His Righteousness;
and all these things shall be added unto you.

The key emphasis again is on seeking the kingdom first. The kingdom must be first. Then God says, "I will add the things." Can you see that?

Now let me explain the principle. God requires faith to react to us. Our works are the forecast of our faith or what we believe. If you really believe your church is going to grow, then the Holy Spirit will begin to instruct you in areas that you need to change. Do not be afraid. Understand that your acceptance must only come from God and living according to his Word. When you need acceptance from others, then you forfeit the voice of God's instructions in your life. Because you are too afraid of what others may say or think.

The people of Noah's day thought he was crazy, but the rain did come. I'm sure the soldiers of Joshua's day thought he had lost it, considering his marching military strategy, but the walls did fall.

So you having faith may push you to an area that you did not intend to be pushed and cause you to encounter scrutiny that you did not expect. However, when the reward of your faith is reached, great joy will set in on your heart. Remember, he is a rewarder of them who diligently seek him. Now let's look at the process of faith.

Process of Faith

For years coming up in a Pentecostal environment, I had been taught to have faith in God. I was taught miracle faith, that God would work miracles if I trusted him. In the environment I grew up in, I have seen saints refusing to go to hospitals, trusting God to heal them.

I remember years ago one precious deacon who had developed a hernia in his lower abdomen. One Saturday morning as I came to prayer, I saw him looking as if he was in pain. I approached and asked him what was wrong. He showed me the hernia and began to explain how painful it was. Then he began to tell me how he was waiting on God to heal him. Well, things got worse, and before long, he was no longer coming to church. He was at home in the bed in severe pain. The saints were praying, and for a couple of days, we thought we were going to lose him.

However, God was merciful and healed his body. I saw with my own eyes that the hernia was gone. We were taught to have this type of faith in God. I like to call it miracle faith. This incident took place at least ten years ago, and that precious deacon is still alive. He never went to the doctor; he just simply trusted God.

However, we were never taught the process of systematic faith. How to believe God for things when your back is not up against a wall. How to believe God when you're not sick or in need of a miracle. What if you needed a new car or dress? How do you believe God to bring this to pass? For purposes of this book, we are asking God to give us membership growth. Once I found about systematic faith, I was so excited because it finally explained to me how to believe in God for the things I desired.

In Mark 11:12, the Bible tells us that Jesus approached a fig tree because he was hungry. The fig tree had nothing but leaves on it. As a result, Jesus cursed the fig tree. He said, "No man eat fruit of you hereafter forever."

In the twentieth verse, the disciples noticed that the tree had dried up from the roots, and they were amazed. Peter brings it to Jesus's attention, saying, "Master, the fig tree you cursed is withered away." Then Jesus replies in the twenty-second and twenty-third verse, saying, "Have faith in God."

> For verily I say unto you, That whosoever shall say unto this mountain, Be thou removed and be thou cast into the sea; and shall not doubt in his heart, but shall believe that those things which he says shall come to pass; he shall have whatsoever he says. Mark 11:23

Now, allow me to put this in my own words. Jesus tells his disciples, "It was not strange that I spoke to the fig tree and the roots obeyed me." He tells them to have faith in God and explains that anyone who speaks to a mountain and tells it to move and shall not doubt in his heart, he will have what he says.

So from this, I learned that the voice of my faith is prayer or what I say that lines up with the Word of God. So prayer becomes the launching pad of my faith. Wow, this certainly changed the way I prayed.

Now let me place emphasis on a portion of verse 23. "But shall believe that those things which he says shall come to pass." If it shall come to pass, that means future tense. The expectation is that it will happen. Now notice what verse 24 says in the same chapter.

> Therefore I say unto you, What things soever you desire, when you pray, believe that you receive them, and you shall have them.

Now Jesus is telling me about my desires. He tells me that I can pray for them. When I pray, I must say something. Some words must come out of my mouth concerning the things that I desire. Please understand God will not fulfill desires that go against his Word. So when it comes to desires, they must not violate the principles of God's Word.

The next emphasis is on the words *when you pray, believe.* This tells me that when I pray, right then I must believe that I have received the thing that I'm asking God for. You must believe, even though you cannot see anything as of yet. This is important because your faith is what it is going to take in order to bring your desires to pass.

Then the scripture says, "You shall have them or the things you prayed for." The emphasis words are *shall have,* meaning at some point in the future, it is coming to pass. Since I believe it and I know it is coming to pass, then I act like it is so. Now the enemy will try to discourage you from believing. So you must be aware of what he does.

He fights us with the time factor. If it does not come to pass as quickly as we desire, then we get discouraged and back up off our faith. I would like to share a story with you about a personal blessing that I stood in faith for and saw it come to pass.

While working for Prudential, I had an opportunity to receive some fairly decent bonuses. One day, I asked God to bless me with a ten-thousand-dollar bonus. I prayed and believed, looking for my production levels to increase. Well, for a while, it appeared that this was some distant dream that would never come to pass for me. In fact, my production level began to drop significantly. So not only does the enemy fight us with time, he fights us because the things we pray for tend to turn in the opposite direction when we stand in faith.

So after my production levels went south, and the time factor was weighing heavily on me, I began to consult the Lord. The Lord impressed upon my heart that faith comes by hearing.

> So then faith cometh by hearing and hearing by the word of God. (Rom. 10:17)

I want to place emphasis on the words *faith comes by hearing*. This was a great revelation to me. I understand how to get faith. So I begin to listen to the Word of God. I wanted to hear it taught to me daily because I wanted to keep my faith high. So there I was, hearing the Word of God, believing God for my bonus. Internally, I really believed it would come to pass.

Faith Props

As I heard the Word, I discovered the power of what I would like to call faith props. I noticed that in Genesis 13:16, God talked to Abraham about the dust of the earth, using the dust of the earth as an example of how God would bless his seed.

Then in Genesis 15:5, I see God telling Abraham to number the stars, again giving him an example of how God would bless.

In Genesis 30:37-43, when Jacob was believing God for increase in cattle, he used faith props. Notice how Jacob used rods of green poplar and of the hazel and chestnut trees and pilled white strakes in them and made the white appear, which was in the rods. And he set the rods that he had pilled before the flocks in the gutters in the watering troughs when the flocks came to drink. The Bible says that the flocks conceived before the rods and brought forth cattle, ring-straked, speckled, and spotted.

Because of what I heard in the Word, I took the scripture Mark 11:24 along with my faith confession of believing God for the ten-thousand-dollar bonus and hung them through my house. I hung them in the bedroom and the bathrooms and confessed them every time I went in or out.

Well, it took some time; it lasted for about six months or more. There were times it appeared that I was simply going through the motions because it did not look like anything was happening. In fact, I had even forgotten about praying the prayer and standing in faith until I would see the signs that I posted in my house.

One day, a gentleman walked into my office at Prudential, requesting to see an agent. I just happened to be the agent there that day. To my surprise, when we sat down to meet, he handed me a very sophisticated portfolio to review. The portfolio was over a million dollars in assets. I promised him I would review it and get back to him in a week's time.

Please bear in mind that we are trained to review a person's total picture before giving advice. This gentleman was not married, neither did he have any children. He was not in need of life insurance, and his portfolio, to say the least, was in fairly decent shape.

I struggled with coming up with a reason that he should do business with me. I even got my manager involved just to get some additional feedback. My manager agreed that we really had no justification for him to allow me to manage his portfolio other than he just needed a change. We did consider that we would save him some tax confusion on his short-and long-term gains tax, but this was minor considering everything.

Well on the day of the next meeting, I was praying and asking God to give me what to say. The Lord impressed upon me to just tell the truth and ask the guy to do business with you. So I explained to him very clearly what we had to offer him. I also explained that it was not much different from what he already had. I told him that the real benefit would be working with me. My manager had told me it would be a miracle if he decided to allow me to manage his portfolio.

After several questions and much consideration, he mentioned to me, "My accountant told me the same thing you explained about short-and long-term gains tax." It was that, just that simple point, that caused this man to do business with me. Under normal circumstances, that would not even be a meaningful discussion, but God had given me favor with this man. He transferred his portfolio to me, which paid me over $14,000 in commissions and a little over $10,000 in a bonus.

As you might imagine, I left work praising God. Not only was this a great faith win, it was the start to many more blessings in my life. I discovered that systematic faith works.

Applying Faith to My Church Growth

Now when I first started pastoring, it was extremely difficult. It was difficult because I did not understand how faith works. Neither did I understand how to apply faith. To be honest, I just started preaching and pastoring with very limited direction. It was like jumping in water and learning how to swim all at the same time.

I think I was like every other pastor; I wanted my church to grow. I loved God; however, my love for God was not enough to cause my church to grow. I needed to learn how to apply and use my faith. Just as I used it for my bonus, now it was time to use faith for church growth.

Humble Beginning

Starting out in a little center located in Oak Park, Illinois, was the best thing that could have ever happen to me. The reason I say that is because it proved very humbling for me. On Sunday mornings, I had to get to the Fox Center early. My job was to let down the chairs, pull out the equipment, and start praying. The hardest part was getting the equipment upstairs, especially the drums. By the time the few people that we had at the time arrived, it appeared that the chairs had already been set up. Little did they know I had arrived early and set everything up.

My lovely wife did the best she could to keep me encouraged every step of the way, and it was just what I needed to keep me going. Even to this very day, I thank God for giving me a good wife.

I remember arriving early one day only to discover the attendant that normally opens the door for us was not there. It was snowing and cold that morning. I started calling every contact number I had just to get someone to open the door, but to no avail. Finally, some of the saints started showing up, and there I was, embarrassed and extremely sad. However, God had surrounded me with good people who were extremely understanding. Finally the attendant arrived, very apologetic that she had overslept. I can truly say God really blessed us this Sunday, as the Holy Ghost fell in a great way. This made my heart glad. The emphasis is the experience of being embarrassed, humiliated, but still having to go on. It helped me appreciate God's people even more. It also made me aware of how much we need to depend upon God.

Getting the "*I*" Out

God has to bring us to the point in ministry where we fall upon our faces and say, "Lord, I am stupid, and I do not know what to do." Simply put, God has to get the *I* out of us. Being in the Fox Center truly helped me rid myself of the *I*. It was then when God began to teach me how to dream.

Every day, I would go in and touch each seat, declaring that it be filled with a born-again believer. Remember, faith is systematic, and over time, I experienced each seat being filled. It took some time, but it happened. People began to come, and it has not stopped, even until this day. I want to encourage you to believe with all of your heart because God is faithful.

There was a time in our ministry we did not have ushers or deacons or a choir. It seemed hopeless at first. Truly, I can see where God has brought us from and where the Lord is taking us.

Learning How to Do Church

It should be the goal of every pastor to learn how to do church. How to properly work ministry at a level that it affects this generation. Ultimately, your pastoral call should be an honorable one, not one of frustration and pain. It can truly be the most rewarding job in the world, to be used by God in a way where people's lives are changed and they grow in the knowledge of our Lord and Savior.

The ingredient that you need most is faith. Look at this scripture found in Hebrews 11:2: "For by faith the elders obtained a good report." That's what working for God is, a good report.

Let's look at another passage of scripture found in Hebrews 10:23: "Let us hold fast the profession of our faith without wavering; for he is faithful that promised." Remember, God is faithful, and he is a rewarder of them who diligently seek him.

I believe with a few minor adjustments, through prayer and your willingness to learn, your church can make a turn today.

Closing Tips

In closing this book, I would like to provide the following tips that I believe will be extremely helpful in your pursuits of church growth.

Tip number one: reorganize and plan every step of the way. In other words, do not be afraid to change things that need to be changed. Ask your membership to have the maturity to flow with change. You must have the support of each member with changes and reorganizing that need to be done.

Tip number two: spend time in the Word of God daily. I believe that every leader should spend at least two hours in Bible study daily. It is a discipline that needs to be developed in the hearts of leaders.

Tip number three: don't be afraid to study what others did to become successful. Study what others did to become successful. This is very important, as it will prove very helpful in expanding your capacity to learn. It may cause you to look outside of your circle, but it is well worth the look.

Tip number four: don't marry any one way. This is important because you don't want to get stuck. Doing things the same way all the time sometimes causes people to get stuck and unwilling to try something new. I am always on the lookout for improvement.

Tip number five: understand your acceptance comes from the Word of God and not other people. Sometimes we can get caught up in other people and lose out on God's direction for us. We only get caught up in other people when we feel a need for acceptance from them. You must be free to move in the direction that God is calling for, even if it puts you at odds with those you love.

Tip number six: take your time and always remember the way up is down. Do not try to be more than what you are too quickly. Allow God to grow you into who he wants you to be.

Tip number seven: guard the anointing on your life from pollution. Remember, the devil is not interested in stopping you from pastoring; he just wants to block your effectiveness.

I am praying for you that this book will stimulate and revitalize your desire to be effective in ministry. One of the true effective measures of ministry is whether or not your church grows. If your church is not growing, then reexamine all areas to determine why you are not being effective. If your church is growing you still should reexamine all areas to strive to be more effective in ministry.

Ministry Need Selected: Would like information about the church?

Step #1 Phone Call

Phone Script: Hello, this is (membership services person) calling from Faith Cathedral Church. May I speak with (person you are calling)? How are you today? I'm calling on behalf of Bishop Dortch to let you know how thankful we were that you chose to worship with us. You made our service very special by your presence.

Step #2 Address Verification

Bishop would like to send you a very special gift, and I just need to verify some information you placed on your special guest card. I will only take a few minutes of your time.

Let me verify your address. (Recite the information off the visitor's card.)

Let me verify your e-mail address. (Recite the information you have on the card.)

Step #3 Verify Ministry Needs

We noticed that you checked off you would like to receive more information regarding our church. Although we have a standard brochure that will provide you the information you are requesting, is there anything specific you would like to know? (Take notes for whatever is said.)

Step #4 Verify E-mail Communication

How often do you read your e-mail?

(If at least once a week) GREAT! Bishop will be preparing a very special video presentation just for you. You don't want to miss it.

(If they don't read their e-mail, then we will mail them a letter with the information they requested.)

Step #5 Closing Remarks

We want you to feel free to attend any of our services. Throughout the year, Bishop will be teaching some exciting Bible series, seminars, and conferences that will truly bless your life. From time to time, you will be receiving information about some of our events. One final thing, Bishop would like to know if you have a special prayer request that you would like him to pray for. _____

_____

All right, we will certainly add this information to our prayer list, and we look forward to worshiping with you again. God bless.

Ministry Need Selected: Would like information about becoming a member?

Step #1 Phone Call

Phone Script: Hello, this is (membership services person) calling from Faith Cathedral Church. May I speak with (person you are calling)? How are you today? I'm calling on behalf of Bishop Dortch to let you know how thankful we were that you chose to worship with us. You made our service very special by your presence.

Step #2 Address Verification

Bishop would like to send you a very special gift, and I just need to verify some information you placed on your special guest card. I will only take a few minutes of your time.

Let me verify your address. (Recite the information off the visitor's card.)

Let me verify your e-mail address. (Recite the information you have on the card.)

Step #3 Verify Ministry Needs

We noticed that you checked off you would like to receive information about becoming a member. As such, Bishop would like to schedule a membership information meeting with you just to explain the benefits you will receive when you become a member. These meetings normally take place on Wednesdays. Would 5:00 p.m. or 6:00 p.m. be better for you? I'm so excited for you, and I know Bishop will be just as excited. (Personal testimony: I can't explain to you how my life has been impacted since I've been at this church.)

Will you need transportation to attend this meeting? (Coordinate as needed.)

* If you set up a meeting, please skip step #4 .

Step #4 Verify E-mail Communication

How often do you read your e-mail?

(If at least once a week) GREAT! Bishop will be preparing a very special video presentation just for you. You don't want to miss it.

(If they don't read their e-mail, then we will mail them a letter with the information they requested.)

Step #5 Closing Remarks

We want you to feel free to attend any of our services. Throughout the year, Bishop will be teaching some exciting Bible series, seminars, and conferences that will truly bless your life. From time to time, you will be receiving information about some of our events. One final thing, Bishop would like to know if you have a special prayer request that you would like him to pray for. _____

All right, we will certainly add this information to our prayer list, and we look forward to worshiping with you again. God bless.

Ministry Need Selected: Would like to meet with the pastor or a minister?

Step #1 Phone Call

Phone Script: Hello, this is (membership services person) calling from Faith Cathedral Church. May I speak with (person you are calling)? How are you today? I'm calling on behalf of Bishop Dortch to let you know how thankful we were that you chose to worship with us. You made our service very special by your presence.

Step #2 Address Verification

Bishop would like to send you a very special gift, and I just need to verify some information you placed on your special guest card. I will only take a few minutes of your time.

Let me verify your address. (Recite the information off the visitor's card.)

Let me verify your e-mail address. (Recite the information you have on the card.)

Step #3 Verify Ministry Needs

We noticed that you checked off you would like to meet with our bishop. As such, Bishop would like to schedule a meeting with you. Just so Bishop is prepared, can you tell me in general what you would like to discuss in the meeting? These meetings normally take place on Tuesdays or Wednesdays, between 2:00 p.m. and 6:00 p.m. Which date and time would be good for you?

Will you need transportation to attend this meeting? (Coordinate as needed.)

* If you set up a meeting, please skip step # 4 .

Step #4 Verify E-mail Communication

How often do you read your e-mail?

(If at least once a week) GREAT! Bishop will be preparing a very special video presentation just for you. You don't want to miss it.

(If they don't read their e-mail, then we will mail them a letter with the information they requested.)

Step #5 Closing Remarks

We want you to feel free to attend any of our services. Throughout the year, Bishop will be teaching some exciting Bible series, seminars, and conferences that will truly bless your life. From time to time, you will be receiving information about some of our events. One final thing, Bishop would like to know if you have a special prayer request that you would like him to pray for._____

All right, we will certainly add this information to our prayer list, and we look forward to worshiping with you again. God bless.

Ministry Need Selected: Would like to know how to improve my life?

Step #1 Phone Call

Phone Script: Hello, this is (membership services person) calling from Faith Cathedral Church. May I speak with (person you are calling)? How are you today? I'm calling on behalf of Bishop Dortch to let you know how thankful we were that you chose to worship with us. You made our service very special by your presence.

Step #2 Address Verification

Bishop would like to send you a very special gift, and I just need to verify some information you placed on your special guest card. I will only take a few minutes of your time.

Let me verify your address. (Recite the information off the visitor's card.)

Let me verify your e-mail address. (Recite the information you have on the card.)

Step #3 Verify Ministry Needs

We noticed that you checked off you would like to know how to improve your life. As such, Bishop has prepared a very special video e-mail presentation just for you. This video e-mail will give you step-by-step instructions based upon the Word of God just how to improve your life. When you receive it, please get in a quiet place so that you can allow the Spirit of God to ministry to you as you listen to the video presentation. (If video e-mail is not possible, then we can send a CD/DVD.)

Step #4 Verify E-mail Communication

How often do you read your e-mail?

(If at least once a week) GREAT! Bishop will be preparing a very special video presentation just for you. You don't want to miss it.

(If they don't read their e-mail, then we will mail them a letter with the information they requested.)

Step #5 Closing Remarks

We want you to feel free to attend any of our services. Throughout the year, Bishop will be teaching some exciting Bible series, seminars, and conferences that will truly bless your life. From time to time, you will be receiving information about some of our events. One final thing, Bishop would like to know if you have a special prayer request that you would like him to pray for. _____

All right, we will certainly add this information to our prayer list, and we look forward to worshiping with you again. God Bless.

Ministry Need Selected: Would like to be placed on the e-mail mailing list?

Step #1 Phone Call

Phone Script: Hello, this is (membership services person) calling from Faith Cathedral Church. May I speak with (person you are calling)? How are you today? I'm calling on behalf of Bishop Dortch to let you know how thankful we were that you chose to worship with us. You made our service very special by your presence.

Step #2 Address Verification

Bishop would like to send you a very special gift, and I just need to verify some information you placed on your special guest card. I will only take a few minutes of your time.

Let me verify your address. (Recite the information off the visitor's card.)

Let me verify your e-mail address. (Recite the information you have on the card.)

Step #3 Verify Ministry Needs

We noticed that you checked off you would like to be placed on our e-mail mailing list. Being a part of our e-mail mailing list will provide you information on all of our upcoming events. In addition to this, when we give out school supplies, Christmas gifts, etc., you will be among the first to receive the invitation.

Step #4 Verify E-mail Communication

How often do you read your e-mail?

(If at least once a week) GREAT! Bishop will be preparing a very special video presentation just for you. You don't want to miss it.

(If they don't read their e-mail, then we will mail them a letter with the information they requested.)

Step #5 Closing Remarks

We want you to feel free to attend any of our services. Throughout the year, Bishop will be teaching some exciting Bible series, seminars, and conferences that will truly bless your life. From time to time, you will be receiving information about some of our events. One final thing, Bishop would like to know if you have a special prayer request that you would like him to pray for. _____

All right, we will certainly add this information to our prayer list, and we look forward to worshiping with you again. God Bless.

Ministry Need Selected: Would like a call from the bishop or a minister of the church?

Step #1 Phone Call

Phone Script: Hello, this is (membership services person) calling from Faith Cathedral Church. May I speak with (person you are calling)? How are you today? I'm calling on behalf of Bishop Dortch to let you know how thankful we were that you chose to worship with us. You made our service very special by your presence.

Step #2 Address Verification

Bishop would like to send you a very special gift, and I just need to verify some information you placed on your special guest card. I will only take a few minutes of your time.

Let me verify your address. (Recite the information off the visitor's card.)

Let me verify your e-mail address. (Recite the information you have on the card.)

Step #3 Verify Ministry Needs

We noticed that you checked off you would like a call from our bishop or a minister. As such, what would be a good time to call you? Is this the number you would like us to call? Our ministry team is looking forward to speaking with you and would like you to be prepared to receive the call.

*Please skip step #5.

Step #4 Verify E-mail Communication

How often do you read your e-mail?

(If at least once a week) GREAT! Bishop will be preparing a very special video presentation just for you. You don't want to miss it.

(If they don't read their e-mail, then we will mail them a letter with the information they requested.)

Step #5 Closing Remarks

We want you to feel free to attend any of our services. Throughout the year, Bishop will be teaching some exciting Bible series, seminars, and conferences that will truly bless your life. From time to time, you will be receiving information about some of our events. One final thing, Bishop would like to know if you have a special prayer request that you would like him to pray for. _____

_____

All right, we will certainly add this information to our prayer list, and we look forward to worshiping with you again. God bless.

INDEX

A

Abraham (father of many nations), 113
Acts
  1:4, *90*
  6:3-4, *38*
  8:30-31, *54*
  13:44, *21*
  16:28-31, *53*
altar call, 24, 66, 74, 78–79, 106
  four parts of, 79
Arthur Andersen, 68

B

Bible class, 11, 28, 31, 36

C

church agenda, 32–33
church growth, 13, 18–19, 26, 90, 98,
  107, 118
church home, 81, 85
church membership
  formal, 87
  spiritual, 87
church misconceptions
  church size, 29
  God increasing membership, 23

  overconfidence in preaching, 24
  overdependence on God, 26
  overdependence on Jesus, 25
church order, 35
conversion growth rate, 9, 61–62
Cornelius (centurion), 54–55
cultivation, 99

D

Daniel (prophet), 30
David (father of Solomon), 18, 28, 75
Dead Sea, 27
Dead Sea scrolls, 31
Derbe, 55
dismissal, 9, 79

E

Ecclesiastes 4:9-12, *37*
Eleazar (priest), 27
Elijah (prophet), 27–28, 109
Elisha (prophet), 27–28
end-time, 31, 76
Ephesians 4:27, *70*
evangelism, 13, 51, 60
  keys to effective, 9, 51
Exodus 18:21, *46*

F

faith, 10, 15, 19, 21, 29, 34, 40, 55, 62,
    64, 74, 81, 88, 103, 107–15, 117
  miracle, 110–11
  systematic, 111, 115
Faith Cathedral Church, 11, 38, 124,
    126, 128, 130
faith goals, 62
Faith Props, 113
faith reaction, 80
fasting, 59, 61, 64, 94, 96
financial responsibility, 42
1 Corinthians
  3:7, *24*
  12:18, *35, 91*
  15:58, *35*
1 Kings
  17:12, *109*
  19:21, *28*
1 Samuel 3:19, *80*
1 Timothy 5:18, *44*
follow-up, 81–82, 89

G

Galilee, Sea of, 27
Genesis
  13:16, *113*
  15:5, *113*
  30:37-43, *113*
growth plan, 9, 58–59

H

Hebrews
  4:12-14, *45*
  6:10, *39*
  10:23, *117*
  10:25, *36*
  11:2, *117*
  11:6, *19, 107*

Holy Ghost, 24, 78–79, 81, 83, 90–91,
    105. *See also* Holy Spirit
Holy Spirit, 54, 75, 78, 90, 110. *See also*
    Holy Ghost

I

invitations, types of
  conviction, 52–53
  divine, 54
  kingdom, 9, 55–57
  opportunity, 53
Isaiah (prophet), 54

J

Jacob (brother of Esau), 113
James
  1:14-15, *93*
  2:14, 17, *108*
Jeremiah
  3:15, *16*
  12:10, *16*
  23:1, *16*
Jesus Christ, 16, 23, 28–29, 32–33,
    57–58, 90–91, 97, 103, 112
Jethro (father-in-law of Moses), 46–47
John
  3:16, *98*
  6:44, *51, 83*
Jordan River, 27
Joshua (servant of Moses), 27, 109
Joshua 6:2, *109*

K

Kingdom of God, 28–29, 75–76, 85, 110

L

law of numbers, 57, 99
law of unity, 37

Luke
  6:38, 44
  14:23, 23, 29, 102
  15:10, 34, 66
  16:10-11, 43
  19:10, 32
  22:26, 39
lust plan, 93, 95
Lydia (seller of purple), 55
Lystra, 55

M

Malachi
  3:6, 41
  3:8, 72
Mark
  11:12, 111
  11:24, 114
  11:25, 15
  16:20, 26, 58, 90
marketing
  external, 104–5
  internal, 104
Matthew
  6:21, 73
  6:33, 109
  24:45-47, 67
  25:23, 29
  28:19-20, 103
  28:36-38, 57
ministry, 5, 11, 16–17, 19, 28–34,
    37–38, 43–44, 47–48, 53, 65–66,
    69–70, 76–78, 103, 105–6, 117,
    119–31
ministry moment, 53, 80, 82
Moody Bible Institute, 83
Moses (prophet), 27, 46–47

N

Noah (builder of the ark), 109–10

O

offerings, 71–72
opening of the service, 68–69
outreach, 13, 22–23, 103, 105
outreach campaign, 101–2

P

passion, 105–6
pastoral giving, 43
pastoring, 12, 15, 20, 115, 119
Paul, Saint (the apostle), 20, 28, 53, 55,
    77, 97
perception, 70, 102
Peter, Saint (the apostle), 54–55, 91,
    111
Philip the Preacher, 54
praying, 23, 64, 66, 96
preaching, 74–76
pride, 20, 91–92
Proverbs
  1:5, 12
  27:2, 92
Psalm 127:1, 18, 64

R

Romans
  7:18-20, 97
  10:17, 113

S

saints, 33–34, 71, 110–11, 116
2 Corinthians
  2:11, 95
  12:7, 20
2 Timothy 2:15, 33, 77
services, 9, 11, 18, 22, 24–26, 35–36,
    38–40, 42–43, 61, 63–71, 75,
    78–81, 84, 88–90, 104–5, 120–31

sexual impurity, 10, 92, 95–96
Silas, Saint, 53
Simon (tanner), 55
social responsibility, 35–36, 67
Solomon (king of Israel), 18, 28

visitors
objects, 50
prospects, 50–51, 59
rejects, 49
suspect, 49

T

team mentality, 44–46
testimonies, 71
Thyatira, 55
Timeliness, 9, 66
Timothy (disciple), 28, 55, 77

W

Word of God, 34, 77, 103, 118, 127

Z

Zarephath, 109

V

visitor card, 82. *See also* visitor form
visitor form, 10, 83. *See also* visitor card

9 781450 037969